OPPORTUNITIES

LIBRARY NEW ENGLAND INST. OF TECHNOLOGY

S0-BAG-295

HF 5547.5 .E78 2007

Ettinger, Blanche.

Opportunities in administrative assistant careers

Administrative Assistant Careers

NEW ENGLAND INSTITUTE OF TECHNOLOGY
LIBRARY

OPPORTUNITIES

in

Administrative Assistant Careers

REVISED EDITION

BLANCHE ETTINGER

NEW ENGLAND INSTITUTE OF TECHNOLOGY
LIBRARY

New York   Chicago   San Francisco   Lisbon   London   Madrid   Mexico City
Milan   New Delhi   San Juan   Seoul   Singapore   Sydney   Toronto

12/10   #71945578

The **McGraw·Hill** Companies

Library of Congress Cataloging-in-Publication Data

Ettinger, Blanche.
  Opportunities in administrative assistant careers / Blanche Ettinger. —Rev. ed.
      p.   cm.
  Rev. ed. of: Opportunities in secretarial careers / Blanche Ettinger. Lincolnwood
(Chicago), Ill. : VGM Career Horizons, c1999. VGM opportunities series.
  ISBN 0-07-147609-1 (alk. paper)
  1. Administrative assistants—Vocational guidance.   2. Office practice—
Vocational guidance.   3. Secretaries—Vocational guidance.   I. Ettinger, Blanche.
Opportunities in secretarial careers.   II. Title.

  HF5547.5.E78   2007
  651.3'7402373—dc22   2006031077

Pages 33, 34, 37–38, 40–41, 96, 138–39: Information provided by the International
Association of Administrative Professionals (IAAP), www.iaap-hq.org.
Page 55: Information provided by Robert Half International, Inc.
Page 57: Data provided by Salary.com™, Inc.
Page 74: NALS Code of Ethics is copyrighted by NALS . . . the association for legal
professionals.

Copyright © 2007 by The McGraw-Hill Companies, Inc. All rights reserved. Printed in the
United States of America. Except as permitted under the United States Copyright Act of
1976, no part of this publication may be reproduced or distributed in any form or by any
means, or stored in a database or retrieval system, without the prior written permission of
the publisher.

1 2 3 4 5 6 7 8 9 10 11 12 13 14 15 16 17 18 19   DOC/DOC   1 0 9 8 7

ISBN-13: 978-0-07-147609-6
ISBN-10:   0-07-147609-1

Interior design by Rattray Design

McGraw-Hill books are available at special quantity discounts to use as premiums and
sales promotions, or for use in corporate training programs. For more information, please
write to the Director of Special Sales, Professional Publishing, McGraw-Hill, Two Penn
Plaza, New York, NY 10121-2298. Or contact your local bookstore.

This book is printed on acid-free paper.

CONTENTS

PREFACE

THIS FOURTH EDITION of *Opportunities in Administrative Assistant Careers* is designed to enlighten you about the changing office environment, employee demographics, impact of the technological revolution on secretarial or administrative assistant positions, and projections for the future. This is an exciting time for you to be a prospective candidate for a position as an office professional. You will become familiar with the many titles of administrative professionals currently in use that reflect the increased responsibilities and expertise contributed to the organization. Your functions not only will be broad in scope, but the procedures you use will be based on established and evolving technologies and their capabilities.

Searching for a job has always been a difficult task, one that today involves even more options through the Internet. The changing workplace has created new jobs, and the continuing advances in technology are sure to create even more. Where will these jobs be and what kind of training will you need? Not only have titles changed for office professionals, but while the traditional skills of oral and written communications, organization, record keeping, time management, and interpersonal relations remain very important, expertise is also necessary in such areas as budgeting, project management, teamwork, negotiating, and advanced computer skills.

To plan for a satisfying and fulfilling career, you need to use an organized and systematic approach. Your first step in this process is self-examination: determine what you really want to be and then evaluate your interests, likes and dislikes, personality, abilities, and shortcomings. When you have a realistic image of yourself and understand the forces that motivate you, you are ready to begin your job search in the specialized field of your choice.

While you are still in school, gain as much knowledge and understanding about society and the business world as you can. Learn about computers and the Internet. Become even more familiar than you probably already are with all forms of office technology and equipment, everything from scanners to printers to videoconferencing equipment. Learn how to develop and transmit an electronic résumé. Also, read in this text about the various types of preliminary interviewing procedures: by telephone, on the Internet, and on-site.

This book reflects the latest developments and trends in the administrative professions and provides data on educational preparation, qualifications, promotional opportunities, salaries, trends, and strategies to use in the job search. The latest information available is also given on the administrative profession in Canada.

After you read this book, you should be able to make informed decisions about your future and plan strategies that will enable you to find a rewarding and challenging career.

Acknowledgments

A SPECIAL THANKS to the many individuals who shared their invaluable comments in the creation of this book to help students bridge the gap between the academic and business worlds.

Many thanks also to Josephine Scanlon for her assistance in preparing this edition.

1

THE CHANGING WORKFORCE

As an administrative assistant, you need to be ready to embrace the challenge of change that has evolved during the last two decades and that affects every aspect of our society: demographic shifts, changing workplace, global economy, office environment, and modes of communication. Computerization and high-tech equipment have given the workplace a new image, altering job descriptions and responsibilities at a revolutionary pace.

What does this mean? It means that to have a successful career as an administrative assistant in the technologically advanced twenty-first century, you must become more skilled in using technology, software, hardware, network systems, multipurpose fax machines, Internet, and e-mail. You will also need to adopt the soft skills: good personal skills, flexibility, responsibility, and a lifelong learning attitude. Office professionals at every level must understand and accept the world in which they work and live and must plan their careers with all the available information about where future jobs will be.

We are living in a very different world—a global economy where the competition is keen, business relationships vary, operational modes differ, and organizations are carefully designed to meet the competition in a timely, effective manner. The aim of this book is to give you a comprehensive overview of the administrative profession so that you will have a greater understanding of this career and the labor market.

Demographic Shifts

People are living longer, and the elderly population is growing. Baby boomers (born between 1946 and 1964) are aging now, and more of them than ever are in the labor force. Ten years ago placement professionals projected that as the average age of the American worker continued to increase, older workers would be experienced and affordable, two qualities prized by employers. This has proven true, as older workers bring experience from past jobs to new positions. In addition, many are working part-time or supplementing pensions from past positions, which means that they may require a lower salary than full-time workers in the prime of their careers.

The U.S. Department of Labor reports that in 2000, 13 percent of the workforce was fifty-five and over, a figure that is expected to increase to 17 percent by 2010. By the year 2050, it is projected that 19 percent of workers will be fifty-five and over. The American Association of Retired Persons (AARP) reports that nearly seven out of ten workers age forty-five to seventy-four tell the AARP that they plan to work in some capacity in retirement.[1]

---

1. American Association of Retired Persons. "The Aging American Workforce: Get Ready," http://www.aarp.org/money/careers/employerresourcecenter/researchanddata/Articles/a2004-07-22-agingworkforce.html, July 25, 2006.

The Bureau of Labor Statistics also reports that the continuing rapid growth of minority groups, particularly Hispanics and Asians, will have a significant impact on the workforce. Immigration, primarily precipitated by the opportunities to find work in the United States, also affected the workforce population as the growth rate of individuals age twenty-five to thirty-four continued to rise.

By 2012, due to faster population growth resulting from a younger population, higher fertility rates, and increased immigration levels, the Hispanic labor force is expected to reach 23.8 million. Despite slower-than-average growth, white non-Hispanics will continue to make up about 66 percent of the labor force.[2]

Workplace

The technology revolution and the global market are two major factors in the transformation of the workplace. Some companies restructured to maintain a focus on what can be done most productively for growth, profit, and competitive advantage. Other organizations eliminated old jobs and developed new job opportunities. Still others have outsourced many positions in an attempt to utilize less-expensive foreign labor forces.

It is much less common today than in the past for workers to stay in the same job for many years. The introduction of new technologies creates new positions, and advancement is dependent on demonstrated skills and abilities. According to a 2005 survey by the International Association of Administrative Professionals (IAAP), almost nine out of ten administrative assistants said they

---

2. Toossi, Mitra. "Labor Force Projections to 2012: The Graying of the U.S. Workforce." *Monthly Labor Review*, February 2004, 127:2, p. 37.

are responding to new job demands by contributing more to their organizations than they were five years ago, and 78 percent said their level of authority and autonomy for decision making has increased as well.[3]

Office of the Future

The office of the future will be increasingly mobile, as technology continues to make it possible for workers to perform their jobs from virtually anywhere. As reported by the IAAP, OfficeTeam, a leading staffing service specializing in highly skilled administrative professionals, has released a report titled *Office of the Future: 2020*.

It should come as no surprise that technology will continue to play a major role in redefining the workplace. Diane Domeyer, executive director of OfficeTeam, says, "Technology will continue to reshape the workplace, changing how and where we conduct business. As a result, flexibility and adaptability will be sought-after attributes in employees at all levels." She adds, "In the future office, there will be added pressure to adapt quickly to change, work smarter, increase productivity and perform duties outside of one's job description. The good news is that emerging technological tools and educational opportunities will better enable professionals to meet these challenges."[4]

---

3. International Association of Administrative Professionals. "Profile of Administrative Professionals," http://www.iaap-hq.org/researchtrends/2005_iaap_profile_of_adminis trative_professionals_survey_results-2.htm, July 14, 2006.

4. International Association of Administrative Professionals. "Office of the Future: 2020," http://www.iaap-hq.org/researchtrends/office_of_future_2020.htm, July 12, 2006.

According to the OfficeTeam study, technology tools should continue to provide even greater flexibility. The use of miniature wireless devices, WiFi, WiMax, and mobile technology will continue to allow employees to work outside the traditional office. Virtual environments and Web-based conferencing services will also provide off-site employees with real-time access to meetings, reducing the need for travel.

Another projection is an increase in telecommuting, as improved wireless connectivity will allow for an increasingly flexible workforce. Nearly 90 percent of the executives surveyed believe that telecommuting will increase in the next ten to fifteen years. While telecommuting makes it possible for employees to work from home, it also challenges their interpersonal skills, as they must build relationships with coworkers while having limited personal interaction.

The advances in wireless technology will also make it possible for more employees to stay in touch with work while on vacation. Many executives think that employees will put in more working hours in the next several years. However, technological advances will make it possible for workers to exert more control over their schedules and establish a better balance between work and life.

New Administrative Roles

The role of administrative assistants will continue to evolve as the workplace continues to change. Careers will become increasingly complex and specialized, and many positions will require sophisticated skills and experience in specific areas such as technology, human resources, and business processes.

Successful administrative assistants will have knowledge of business management principles, technical aptitude, strong interpersonal skills, and a good understanding of the needs of the organization. Business-focused training that emphasizes negotiation, delegation, budgeting, supervision, and planning skills will be valuable. Other areas in which knowledge will be useful are desktop publishing for the creation of newsletters, presentation materials, and other corporate documents; library science for organizing and storing text and data used by groups; and electronic communications for ensuring the security and integrity of electronically transmitted information.

In the next ten to fifteen years, administrative assistants are expected to function more as specialists than generalists, with job descriptions focusing on the technical and managerial aspects of daily business operations.

As secretaries have evolved into administrative assistants, even that title is likely to change to better describe the greater specialization of administrative assistants in the future. Following are some examples of anticipated functions in the office of the future.

- **Resource coordinator.** As companies rely more on contract workers, the resource coordinator will have to bring together the right human resources for a project.
- **Workflow controller.** This professional will function as the control center of an organization, ensuring that the project teams assembled by the resource coordinator have the support and resources required to do their jobs. The workflow coordinator will also facilitate interaction among teams and coordinate the use and transfer of company resources.
- **Knowledge manager.** To ensure continuity and consistency, and to help new employees adapt to the organization's culture, the knowledge manager will function as a repository of institutional

information, history, and best practices. Functioning similarly to a librarian, this staff member will assist workers in locating documents or data.

- **Telecommuting liaison.** Companies will require this position to connect remote workers with each other and with management. Responsibilities will include managing telecommuting schedules and providing technical support and updates to telecommuters, as well as working with senior management to develop policies.
- **Virtual meetings organizer.** This employee will help workers schedule conferences and set up necessary equipment. The organizer will be technically proficient and trained in the use of cameras, projection systems, electronic whiteboards, meeting software, audio equipment, and related tools.

Based on their research, OfficeTeam and industry experts have identified six skills that office professionals will need to prepare for successful careers in this new environment. They form the acronym ACTION:

1. *Analysis.* Analyzing information and exercising good judgment
2. *Collaboration.* Establishing rapport and facilitating team building
3. *Technical aptitude.* Selecting the best technical tools and using them effectively
4. *Intuition.* Identifying and adapting to the needs and work styles of others
5. *Ongoing education.* Engaging in continual learning
6. *Negotiation.* Participating in business discussions that produce positive results

It is expected that careers in the secretarial field will continue to evolve, becoming increasingly complex and specialized. The office of the future will become increasingly mobile and flexible, with core teams managing employees working from such diverse locations as home offices and temporary business spaces. Successful employees will be those who have a combination of technical and interpersonal skills and who can adapt quickly to change.

U.S. Economy and Employment Data

According to the Congressional Budget Office (CBO), the U.S. economy continued to expand at a healthy pace during 2005. According to CBO's projections, inflation (as measured by the consumer price index for urban consumers) was expected to be 2.5 percent in 2006, compared with 2.7 percent in 2004, and it is projected to average 2.2 percent annually in 2007 through 2015. The unemployment rate will remain at a steady, average 5.2 percent from 2005 through 2015, slightly lower than the 5.5 percent rate in 2004.

The foreign trade sector is still expected to remain the fastest-growing component of the gross domestic product. Private investment is also expected to remain a substantial part of the economy. The fundamental factor in the growth of foreign trade and private investment is the expanding business in high technology and in computer-related products. Therefore, as an office professional in a knowledge-based economy, it is important that you develop your competencies for growth and mobility in a global economy.

Employment Projections

The job market for the past decade has had uninterrupted growth. In mid-2006, the civilian labor force was 151.3 million strong, with total employment of 144.4 million. The greatest gains continue to be in the areas of technology and health services.

Through 2012, employment in office and administrative support occupations is projected to increase by 1.6 million but to grow slowly. The category of administrative support occupations, including clerical, is projected to have an employment level of 25.4 million workers in 2012, up from 23.8 million in 2002. Although the number of workers is expected to increase by only 1.6 million jobs, or 8 percent, it is a field of work to be considered.

More than a quarter of these new jobs are expected to be in rapidly growing employment services that provide employees to other industries on a contract or fee basis. A quarter of new jobs are projected for the health care and social assistance industries, and one in six for professional, scientific, and technical services.

In almost all industries, advances in office technology and electronic business are expected to have a growth rate lower than overall employment. The continuing practice of businesses to use temporary workers should also add to this trend. Although this decline is expected to affect word processors and secretaries (except legal, medical, and executive), a relatively large growth rate is projected for occupations with more personal interaction, such as receptionists and information clerks, and bill and account collectors, who are less affected by technology.[5] If you want to be an administrative professional, you should develop your administrative and human relation skills in conjunction with the required computer skills so that you can assume the higher-level responsibilities expected of office professionals today. Read the current job

---

5. Hecker, Daniel E. "Occupational Employment Projections to 2012." *Monthly Labor Review,* February 2004, 127:2, p. 99.

ads for an overview of titles, requirements, and firms where employment positions are available.

Multiple Positions

Multiple jobholders add millions of jobs to the economy and are significant to an analysis of the labor market. According to the Bureau of Labor Statistics, in June 2006 the number of persons who held more than one job decreased by 320,000, to 7.4 million. This group accounted for 5.1 percent of total employment, down from 5.4 percent a year earlier.

More than half combined a full-time job with a part-time one; one in five combined two part-time jobs. The percentage of women who held part-time jobs was two and a half times greater than the number of men who worked two or more part-time jobs.

It is interesting to note that the percentage of individuals holding multiple positions increased with education. Generally, wages were higher, too. However, these factors did not contribute to the reasons for working at more than one job. Besides financial reasons for holding multiple positions, individuals with more education may have the skills and knowledge sought by employers. Those with secretarial and administrative skills can often find second jobs, since many smaller offices and businesses require the services of part-time workers.

Canadian Economy and Workforce

According to Statistics Canada, by the end of 2005 employment increased by 216,000, more than double the growth in the first half of 2005, to a total of over 16.5 million. Unemployment was at a thirty-two-year low of 6.1 percent. The first half of 2006 saw above-average employment gains in the industries of finance, insurance, real estate and leasing, health care and social assistance, natural resources, and other service professions.

Two-way trade of goods, services, and income on investments between Canada and the United States has continued to increase, and Canada has experienced much success and growth in environmental, telecommunications, and information technologies.

As a result of significant investments in services, technology, equipment, and new methods of production, the Canadian economy, like that of the United States, is undergoing tremendous changes. Also, like most economically advanced countries, the fastest, most remarkable growth has been in the service sector, which accounts for the largest number of jobs and a shortage of flexible, skilled workers. Taking into account the entire population employed in retail and wholesale trade, finance, and transportation, as well as public and federal service employees, approximately two-thirds of all Canadians are employed in the service sector. In the administrative support occupational category of the public service sector, 85 percent of workers were women. Overall employment in office occupations is expected to show little growth and may even see a slight decline; however, employment growth is expected in areas such as professional business services, private law practices, hospitals, and medical laboratories.

More individuals age fifty-five to sixty-four were working later in life and spending less time in leisure activities in 2005. Both men and women were spending roughly an hour a day more in paid work than they were in 1998.

2

Nature of Administrative Assistant Positions

THE OPPORTUNITIES FOR administrative assistant careers continue to grow and offer a bright future. They are the largest segment of the office workforce: 4.1 million people are employed as administrative specialists in the United States. In Canada, 476,000 administrative assistants are employed, including 365,670 secretaries. According to the U.S. Department of Labor, more than 184,000 administrative assistant and secretarial positions will be added between 2002 and 2012, representing growth of 4.5 percent.

Numerous job openings will result from the need to replace workers who transfer to other occupations or leave this very large occupation for other reasons each year. Opportunities should be best for those with extensive knowledge of software applications and for experienced administrative assistants. Projected employment varies by occupational specialty. Growing industries, such as administrative and support services; health care and social assistance; educational services (private); and professional, scientific, and technical services will continue to generate most new job opportunities. Legal, medical, and executive secretaries, who account for about 47 percent of all secretaries and administrative assistants, should have good job opportunities throughout the projection period.

Increasing office automation and organizational restructuring will continue to make administrative assistants more productive in coming years, as computers, e-mail, scanners, and voice-message systems allow them to accomplish more in the same amount of time.

Also, with corporate and workforce restructuring, administrative duties have been altered, expanded, or reassigned. If this occurs in your job, stay calm, set goals, determine what skills you must acquire, and get the training needed to assume your new responsibilities. Keep in mind that while restructuring might initially seem upsetting, you can view it as a positive experience, as an opportunity to learn new skills and explore different areas of work.

In the past, secretaries generally worked for one individual or in a pool. In today's workforce, it is more common for managers and professionals to share administrative assistants. However, presidents of corporations, partners of legal firms, and CEOs still require a highly skilled secretary to perform the responsibilities of the position. According to the International Association of Administrative Professionals (IAAP), 54 percent of secretaries support more than one executive, 26 percent support three or four executives, and 11 percent support from five to ten.

If you are considering a career as a secretary or administrative assistant, you should be aware of trends that affect the nature of the work and the competencies required for positions in automated offices. Although our highly technological and competitive world will continue to expand, bringing about further changes in the work environment, set your goals not only for mastery of the technical skills but for the personal, administrative, communicative, and interactive skills that cannot be replaced by equipment. For example, a busy executive should not have to spend time dealing with the 20 percent of voice mail and e-mail messages that are junk. Software cannot understand office politics or differentiate between such junk and important information that needs the manager's attention. Technology could never rival the sophisticated judgment of a human administrative assistant.

In Canada, office automation is redefining the role of the secretary into that of information worker. The growth of the service industry, technological innovation, and changing procedures are transforming both the nature of jobs and the skills required to do them. Employers are now seeking employees with the following competencies: computer expertise, knowledge of word processing software packages, ability to transcribe documents, basic academic competence, analytical and problem solving abilities, communication and interpersonal skills, initiative, creativity, and adaptability.

From Secretaries to Managers

The professional secretary has become a part of the management team. Today, these workers no longer handle just the routine duties of typing, filing, and copying but have become decision makers and provide the links between the different parts of the organization. They are increasingly handling tasks previously performed by managers and other professionals.

In a 2005 survey by the International Association of Administrative Professionals, respondents said the areas in which their responsibilities have shown the most growth are office management and information coordination and supervision. Responsibilities also increased in travel planning, meeting planning, project management, and online purchasing. Administrative staff also report greater involvement in budget development and expense tracking.[1]

Several of the duties mentioned above were once handled by displaced middle managers, making today's administrative assistant a goal-oriented manager. As attitudes and expectations of administrative personnel and management continue to evolve, we should consider the changing roles of administrative assistants.

Following are several managerial roles frequently filled by administrative personnel.

- **Information manager.** Handles paper records and the organization's electronic files and databases; develops methods for organizing and retrieving records
- **Communications manager.** Writes and edits materials including in-house publications and manuals, and may also write or contribute to press releases
- **Inventory manager.** Monitors inventory levels and condition of equipment and develops specifications for purchase of products
- **Planning manager.** Keeps tabs on details relating to projects
- **Logistics manager.** Handles travel, meeting schedules, and agendas
- **Policy manager.** Maintains company manual and interprets policies and procedures to employees

---

1. International Association of Administrative Professionals. "Profile of Administrative Professionals," http://www.iaap-hq.org/researchtrends/2005_iaap_profile_of_adminis trative_professionals_survey_results-2.htm, July 14, 2006.

- **Employee relations manager.** Interviews and hires and acts as supervisor to less-senior staff
- **Financial manager.** Prepares and approves vouchers and financial correspondence
- **Community relations manager.** Solves customer needs and problems
- **Training manager.** Provides guidance on workplace skills
- **Action manager.** Organizes the boss's workload

Mobility

Many career paths are being created for workers in office/administrative professions. For ambitious individuals, a secretarial position is a stepping-stone to a higher-level job.

Secretaries and administrative assistants generally advance by being promoted to other administrative positions with more responsibilities. Qualified administrative assistants who broaden their knowledge of a company's operations and enhance their skills may be promoted to senior or executive secretary or administrative assistant, clerical supervisor, or office manager.

Secretaries with word processing or data-entry experience can advance to jobs as word processing or data-entry trainers, supervisors, or managers within their own firms or in a secretarial, word processing, or data-entry service bureau. Secretarial and administrative support experience also can lead to jobs such as instructor or sales representative with manufacturers of software or computer equipment. With additional training, many legal secretaries become paralegals.

Secretaries have become invaluable to some employers who are reluctant to show approval of a promotion because they don't want to lose their secretaries, who frequently are their confidantes and someone to bounce things off of. A director of a museum stated, "Just for the sheer volume of information and knowledge of the running of the museum, the history of the museum, and the thousands of people involved in making the museum go, she is invaluable."

Developments in office technology are sure to continue at a rapid pace, and they will further change the secretary's work environment. The kind of work performed in today's office can be best described by using technical terms such as *integration, cyberspace, networked office, multimedia, infrastructure, website, NT server, audio-* and *videoconferencing, browser, search engines,* and *digital communication.* As new systems and modes of operation occur, new titles will emerge reflecting the higher levels of skills necessitated by the changing nature of the job. Currently, secretaries are known by different designations, too, which reflect the increased responsibilities assumed in the office.

Viewpoints of Administrative Professionals

Viewpoints from various experienced professionals in the field on the expanding, multifaceted role of the administrative assistant are presented here to give you a better understanding of secretarial work as a career. Through their statements run a common understanding that as secretarial positions become more challenging, secretaries are taking on bigger roles; they are assuming higher-level decision-making responsibilities, which are reflected in the new titles that are emerging. Education beyond high school in computers, oral presentation, and written skills is becoming a prerequisite for advancement.

Sharon A. Stewart has worked as an administrative secretary at a real estate firm for more than twenty years. She still remembers that her employer told her she would learn many things on the job, and the most complex facet would be about people. After many years of experience, she supports that statement and says, "He did not exaggerate!"

Stewart notes that the most striking difference she has seen in her years with the company is the manual office. "The bookkeeping, record keeping, ledgers, rent bills, invoices, etc., were all done by hand," she says. "No computers, no fax machine, no answering machine, and no backup. Just me! Looking back, I am amazed that it all got done." Today she accomplishes the same tasks using specialized software packages designed for the real estate industry.

She recommends that you be prepared and know how to manage your time to be successful in an administrative secretarial career. Time management is invaluable, and knowing how to prioritize is the ultimate office tool.

Stewart has always considered herself a professional and has worked at conducting herself in a courteous and professional manner, whether in dealings with her boss, the tenants, or the plumber. Although her job is secretary, she has also had to be a diplomat, a referee, and even the scapegoat.

She feels that a good experience on a job will result in growth of knowledge and enhancement of capabilities. She says, "To a company, you are an asset and are contributing to its productivity. Make your job a continuous learning experience."

Karen A. Sullivan has worked as an administrative professional in different industries. She began her career working in a small private hospital as secretary to the director of the cardiopulmonary department. Shorthand was an important skill in this position, because Sullivan was responsible for taking notes to enter into patients' charts. Her duties included scheduling appointments and interacting with the other departments.

Sullivan next worked for a company that promoted musical talent. As executive assistant to the owner, she managed his calendar and made travel arrangements for both her boss and some influential clients. She handled extensive correspondence and was responsible for ensuring that scheduled events went off successfully. She used databases and spreadsheets to coordinate events and prioritize work for her boss.

In her next position, she worked in the front office of an exclusive golf club/residential community. Here Sullivan greeted visitors, handled event planning, and interacted with vendors and residents. She used spreadsheets regularly to keep track of events and conducted Internet research. Sullivan sees the common thread among all of her jobs, aside from the straight secretarial functions, as the ability to interact with people at all levels, both within the organization and outside it. She stresses the need to consider interpersonal skills as important as professional skills.

Barbara G. Pollack worked as the occupational education chairperson at a midsized public high school for more than ten years. After retiring from this position, she decided to apply her knowledge to a career in the business world, which has given her very broad experiences with major companies such as IBM, Con Edison, and Citibank.

Pollack believes it is important for administrative assistants to keep up with changing office trends, especially technological advances. She suggests that another good way to remain up-to-date is to work as an office temp in the corporate world. If you plan to work for a temporary agency, Pollack advises that you have a résumé ready to submit and be prepared to take tests in keyboarding, grammar, math, or computer operations. Major temporary employment agencies may even have self-paced software to train you on various software programs. If you score well on the test after training, the agency might get a trainer for you so that you can continue learning the equipment to apply for a higher-level job. With the appropriate skills, the agencies will send you out frequently for a job if you dress in corporate business attire, demonstrate common sense and maturity, and possess advanced computer skills.

Based on her experience, Pollack knows that in large corporations you may be asked to orient new employees to the job. She suggests writing everything down when you get your own orientation. Then write a job description with how-tos to share with the permanent employees, so that they can carry out their duties without excessive questioning. Familiarize yourself with the organizational chart of the department in which you work and have a place for important phone numbers, the code for the department, and the names of persons with whom you have contact.

Pollack recommends keeping a neat workstation and putting things away each evening. Learn how your manager wants work returned for signature; learn how to pick up documents after your superior has looked at them and marked them for distribution, filing, or scheduling. Become familiar with the company's phone system, particularly transferring calls. Find out whether your manager prefers that you send calls directly or screen them first.

Pollack also suggests that you take advantage of all in-service training the company offers. If your company pays for college courses, take them. Joining local professional organizations is a good way to network with others, which will help you to stay on the cutting edge and become more valuable to your organization. On the job, you need to score as close as possible to 100 percent accuracy for everything you do. It is a good idea to team up with a coworker, if possible. Be friendly to everyone, and learn about your community to be prepared for setting up an outside luncheon or to direct a visitor to your office from a train, a plane, or the highway.

These statements reflect the need for administrative assistants who are challenged and who will be able to cope with the higher-level responsibilities that require thinking individuals who can make decisions, manage and execute projects, manipulate and manage information, and enhance office operations. Undoubtedly those with the appropriate background, skills, knowledge, and motivation to learn will have many career opportunities in the years ahead.

Historical Growth of Professional Secretaries

To understand the modern role of the professional secretary, it is necessary to trace the evolution of the office. An understanding of the past coupled with the present will give you a better grasp of what is yet to come.

The earliest civilizations of Greece had need for secretaries (also known as confidants) to handle correspondence and to record historical, business, private, and public information. Shorthand was mastered by such Roman leaders as Julius Caesar and the Emperor Augustus. In Italy and France, it was used until the seventh century A.D., when people began to mistrust it, and it disappeared into the cloisters during the Middle Ages. During the Renaissance, from 1400 to 1500, several shorthand systems were developed in England, initially with religious terms, to be followed by legal, political, and finally commercial words. In the early days in the

United States, in contrast to the current female-dominated secretarial positions, men dominated the office, performing stenographic and bookkeeping tasks. This was considered a position with distinction and status and from which these men could be elevated to higher positions. "Personal" or "private" preceded the word *secretary* to reflect this status. In the United States, John Quincy Adams, Henry Adams, John Hay, and Lyndon Johnson were some of our great leaders who began their careers as secretaries to important political persons.

It was not until Christopher Sholes invented the typewriter in 1867 and perfected it in 1873 that shorthand increased in use. Together, they became communication tools. About this time, women very slowly began to enter the office in stenographic positions, and private business schools began to flourish. Contrary to current statistics, originally men and boys were students. It wasn't until the beginning of the twentieth century that the majority of trainees were women.

It is also interesting to note that when men were working as private secretaries, the position was a prestigious one, but as soon as women began to assume this role, a reversal in image occurred. There was obvious discrimination against women, who received much less pay than men for the same long hours, yet were expected to conduct themselves properly and with loyalty. Women filled the void created by the expansion of industry and the growth of paperwork. They adapted to the technology of the time and learned how to operate typewriters, telephones, transcribing machines, and calculation machines.

By the 1930s, women dominated the office workforce and once again kept pace with technology by learning the electric typewriter. A small group of women who had foresight and vision recognized the importance of continuing education and became the charter members of the Professional Secretaries International (now the International Association of Administrative Professionals), organized in 1942. The Institute for Certifying Secretaries, a group responsible for certifying examinations for secretaries, was formed in 1951.

The next major breakthrough occurred in the mid-1960s, with the introduction by IBM (International Business Machines Corporation) of the Magnetic Tape Selectric Typewriter. Automatic deletion and insertion of words, storage, and flawless and random access printing became a reality. This was the beginning of our modern concept of word processing. Some subsequent inventions that had an impact on secretarial positions were the IBM Mag Card in 1973, memory typewriters, stand-alone word processors, video display terminals, microprocessing and telecommunications technology, desktop computers, modems, optical character readers, networked systems, integrated information systems, and others. The introduction of advanced technology led to transformations in office structures, organization, position responsibilities, and work environments.

In the information era of the 1990s, office environments were changing very rapidly, and secretaries, once again, had to meet the challenges of the new explosion of technology. Personal computers were appearing on the desks of executives, secretaries, and other office support staff in both large and small offices.

The new generation of computer technology enhanced the flow of information and processed data at much faster speeds. Greater responsibilities imposed on secretaries were the maintenance of databases, development of spreadsheets, integration of text and graphics to produce professional-looking documents, and preparation of presentation graphics, including charts, that were attractive and dramatic. Software became more sophisticated. In the last half of the 1990s, the Internet, World Wide Web, and videoconferencing became important business and household tools. Today, tremendous numbers of people are in front of a keyboard—some for extended periods of time, particularly when they go into chat rooms or do research. This factor certainly supports the need to be efficient at the keyboard.

There is interesting research being conducted to develop sophisticated voice output devices that would enable the computer to recognize the user's voice. Many systems are in use but need more sophistication in understanding dialects and pronunciation. The system must be highly responsive to different voices. Several speech recognition systems are now available that "know" thirty thousand words. Hundreds of thousands of people use voice recognition when they place a call and respond to the recorded voice!

Research is still being done on discrete speech input, which requires the user to pause between words, and the natural speech input, which allows the person to talk in any manner.

Can you imagine what tomorrow will bring? Administrative assistants will continue to forge ahead and meet the challenges as they have in the past.

Administrative Professionals Week

Administrative Professionals Week was instituted in 1952 as Professional Secretaries Week by Professional Secretaries International (originally called the National Secretaries Association and now known as the International Association of Administrative Professionals) with a proclamation by Charles Sawyer, Secretary of Commerce. The purpose of this forward-looking group was to uplift the image of the secretary from one of servitude to recognition of "the American secretary upon whose skills, loyalty, and efficiency the functions of business and government offices depend." Today, the purpose of Administrative Professionals Week, which is observed annually the last full week in April, is twofold: ". . . to increase public awareness of the vital role played by secretaries in business, industry, education, government, and the professions; and to reaffirm the dedication of secretaries to professional performance of their responsibilities." During this week, local chapters sponsor seminars and workshops while some members speak to educational, professional, and civic groups. Noted governmental officials have acknowledged the valuable contributions of professional secretaries.

In observance of Administrative Professionals Week, Elnar G. Hickman, past president of Professional Secretaries International, believed this was an appropriate time to "rededicate ourselves to proclaiming the tremendous potential a secretarial career offers." She believes that ". . . the secretarial profession is a way to make a living, a way to make a life, and a way to make a difference." Thus Administrative Professionals Week is a time to show respect and recognition. Administrative personnel would like to see this week of recognition change from an occasion for lunch with the boss or a bouquet of flowers to an increase in responsibilities and activities as part of the management team.

Quality of Employees

Quality improvement, a concept always related to the production process, is now becoming important in white-collar work throughout the nation. The application of this concept to knowledge jobs, such as that of the administrative assistant, was practiced by the Japanese for several decades before it was finally adopted by the United States to maintain its competitive edge against foreign markets. Companies that are adopting such programs are involving all office employees in their search for ways to improve quality of process. Knowledge workers become aware that the task they perform is part of a total process that serves the customer. They are becoming involved in quality circles where they discuss problems, brainstorm for innovative techniques that benefit both the company and themselves, make decisions, and interrelate with their peers.

Characteristics of Administrative Assistants

Regardless of the industry in which you are employed, you will need certain qualities to be a successful administrative assistant. Given what you have already read about the changing workplace, you can see that acquiring skills in new and emerging technology is extremely important. A strong working knowledge of a variety of integrated software applications, Internet communications, and research skills will be beneficial.

Your training as an administrative assistant will provide you with broader skills than those previously associated with secretarial work. Your responsibilities might include training, accounting, information management, and negotiation. Your strong interpersonal skills will be a tremendous advantage in these areas.

The ability to work autonomously is also becoming more important. This means that you will have less direct interaction with bosses and more with clients and employees in other departments. It also includes being able to make decisions independently and manage your own work and schedule. Closely related to this is the ability to take the initiative and not wait to be asked to do something. Meet your deadlines and goals.

Since you'll need to be able to work autonomously, you should also be able to find the most effective and time-efficient ways of getting the job done. It will be up to you to set your priorities and to be able to manage several tasks simultaneously.

As part of a management team, you'll have to work productively with other members of your department as well as with other staff throughout the company. You will also be interacting with all levels of management, and here again your diplomacy, tact, and personality will help you to succeed.

Keep in mind that as rapidly as changes have occurred in the last few years, they will only continue to do so. Technology marches on, and it will be up to you to keep pace. Take advantage of educational opportunities, especially those offered by your company. Join professional organizations that allow you to network with other professionals, and utilize their training options.

Remember that the skills you bring to your job are vital to your employer's success. A company can't run without dedicated, experienced, and ambitious administrative assistants.

3

ORGANIZATIONAL STRUCTURE AND CLIMATE

ADMINISTRATIVE ASSISTANTS MAKE decisions about employment opportunities based on the job itself, the organizational structure, and the physical environment of the company. Changes have occurred in each of these areas due to increased competition that forced business restructuring or downsizing.

Workplace trends have stimulated conversions in the organizational structure, office environment, and ways in which office workers perform their jobs. In this chapter you will become familiar with the ever-changing character of the modern office and the new work culture that has flourished, resulting from advanced and highly sophisticated technology, innovative business practices, and alternative work styles that have impacted the traditional role of the secretary.

It might seem hard to believe that in their original office use, computers were basically tools for word processing. Today, it's difficult to imagine any office functioning without a computer, from a Fortune 500 company to your dentist's office. Employees use computers to handle multitasking and incorporate programs such as database management, spreadsheets that perform mathematical calculations, and graphics to create artwork in many forms, including data and words. Most important, computers have also evolved into communication tools that are an integral part of both small and large businesses. The technology has changed the attitudes of office staff and the way in which many tasks are performed. Modems and cellular phones can turn any environment into workspace.

In conjunction with these trends, the emphasis is no longer solely on automating corporate headquarters but rather on the virtual office, which might be a home office or a mobile office where work is performed. Companies recognize the need for private space in which individuals can read, think, and accomplish tasks, as well as a place where employees can team up with their colleagues for discussions and decision making. To achieve this, an open plan is often used, employing movable partitions and acoustical screens. The individual employees' workstations are also self-contained.

Since the traditional secretarial body of knowledge has expanded tremendously, increased opportunities for upward mobility will be available only to those who make the effort to become broadly educated and acquire the skills and personal qualities necessary to function as a valued member of the company.

Office Information Systems

Technology has allowed the greatest changes in the office environment, and its progress shows no sign of slowing down. As computers get smaller, as cell phones perform more and more functions, and as personal communication devices become more sophisticated, the way our offices function will continue to evolve.

Office information systems are designed to improve the effectiveness of an organization by automating routine procedures, maintaining good records, facilitating communications, and offering timely customer services. Word processing, databases, spreadsheets, calendaring, desktop publishing, records management, and e-mail are basic components of these office information systems. Groupware is a more recent trend that enables employees to collaborate on projects.

Other subsystems of office information systems are transaction processing systems (to maintain records of all transactions); management information systems, or MIS (to generate reports from the data produced by transaction processing systems); and decision support systems, or DSS (to manipulate data pertinent to problems for decision making).

Administrative assistants, supervisors, managers, and executives are dependent on office automation to perform their tasks. Many corporations use integrated, networked systems. As an administrative assistant you will need to keep abreast of the latest technology. You are probably familiar with many of the definitions below that describe components of office systems.

- **Applications software.** Software enabling the user to perform specific tasks on the computer: word processing, spreadsheets, desktop publishing, and personal information management
- **Calendaring.** A way to keep track of meetings and special events on a computer calendar
- **Computer program.** A set of detailed instructions that enables a computer to perform a task

- **Database.** A collection of systematically organized data or information that is stored and retrieved for various purposes
- **Desktop publishing.** The ability to combine text and graphics to produce reports, brochures, newsletters, and other publications of nearly the same quality as those produced by commercial print shops
- **Electronic mail.** Computerized information sent over telephone wires, cables, or satellites
- **E-mail.** A message sent electronically from one user to another
- **Extranet.** An Intranet environment that has controlled access for public users such as authorized customers and vendors
- **Groupware.** Software designed to help people collaborate on projects
- **Internet.** A collection of networks linked together around the world to exchange data and distribute processing tasks
- **Intranet.** A private network in a company that enables employees to access the Internet
- **Multimedia.** The integrated use of computer-based media, including graphics, sound, animation, video, and images
- **Multitasking.** A process where you run two or more programs at a time
- **Network.** Interconnection of a number of computers by communication facilities
- **Spreadsheet.** An intersecting grid of rows and columns that resembles the accountant's worksheet and is used for presenting numerical information and formulas in a matrix of cells
- **Telecommunications.** An electronic method for communicating messages over telephone lines
- **Wi-Fi.** Wireless Internet access that allows users with appropriate devices, such as computers, telephones, or personal digital

assistants (PDAs), to connect to the Internet when in proximity of an access point

• **Windowing.** A function that splits the screen into two or more parts, allowing information from one document to be displayed in another

Evolving Job Titles of Administrative Assistants

In the past, employees working in an office were known as *receptionists*, *clerks*, or *secretaries* (general, executive, legal, or medical). People in these positions generally used typewriters, transcribing machines, and duplicators to perform their tasks. The usual responsibilities included typewriting, filing, and duplicating materials. Although the titles of these office workers may still be used, the position has changed as well as the nature of the job. Secretaries have become much more productive since computers, fax machines, scanners, and e-mail arrived. However, there are many duties of the position that are of a personal nature and cannot be automated, such as working with clients and planning meetings and conferences.

Some of the titles being used today include *secretary*, *executive assistant*, *executive secretary*, *administrative secretary*, *administrative assistant*, and *office manager*. However, in a recent survey[1] of members of the International Association of Administrative Professionals (IAAP), fewer than half the respondents indicated that their titles included the word *secretary*. Instead, the more commonly

---

1. "The 21st Century Administrative Professional," International Association of Administrative Professionals, http://www.iaap-hq.org/researchtrends/21centuryadmin.htm, July 13, 2006.

used job titles include terms such as *coordinator*, *administrator*, *specialist*, and *associate*.

Administrative Job Titles

Administrative assistant	30%
Executive assistant	18%
Executive secretary	6%
Office manager or supervisor	5%
Secretary	5%

A review of the "Job Market" section of the *New York Times* on a recent weekend revealed thirty-four advertisements for administrative assistants, four for executive assistants, and one for secretary. This is a clear indication of the evolution of secretaries into administrative assistants and related office professionals.

The importance of job titles is outlined in an article published by the IAAP. Your job title can affect your compensation, promotional opportunities, and prestige. The following are several things to keep in mind about job titles when you are upgrading your job description, negotiating for a new job, or considering changing positions.[2]

• Some companies use clearly defined job titles and descriptions, but others (usually smaller ones) allow executives and assistants to determine the job title.

---

2. Fenner, Susan. "'A Rose By Any Other Name' Does Not Apply to Job Titles." International Association of Administrative Professionals, http://www.iaapphq.org/research trends/job_titles_rose_by_any_other_name.htm, July 16, 2006.

- Be aware of titles that might dead-end your options. Titles that could be refreshed and updated are *clerk, receptionist, data entry*, and *transcriptionist*.
- A new title may increase your earnings if you are at the top of your pay scale.
- References to technology are useful, such as *desktop publisher, graphics designer, multimedia specialist*, and *network administrator*.
- Review industry surveys to see which categories pay the most, and adapt your title to match them.
- If you cannot change your classification, see if you can add a descriptor. For example, *secretary* might be changed to *secretary II* or *senior secretary*.
- Use words that describe administrative work, such as *coordinator, assistant, representative*, and *manager*.
- To be promoted within a certain area, use that field in your title. For instance, if you seek a promotion in marketing, the title *marketing assistant* is stronger than *administrative assistant*.
- Be sure that your résumé shows a progression in titles, such as a move from *administrative assistant* to *administrative manager*.
- Try to use a title that encompasses the total job, such as *communications specialist, information coordinator*, or *assistant to the director*.

Modern Office Technology

The impact of technology on the office environment is apparent in the way work is performed, where it is done, how information is accessed, how computer-generated information is transported, and how communications are exchanged. New equipment and systems to increase productivity and reduce costs have been introduced;

new services and strategies have been developed; and new positions have evolved. Other major changes occurred with the restructuring of the organization and downsizing, which did affect the worker and the workplace.

The driving forces behind most of these changes are the computer, the ever-increasing power of the microchip, and telecommunications. You need to be computer literate, be knowledgeable about software and hardware, understand communications systems and workplace organization, and be familiar with procedures and the office environment as you plan your administrative career in information systems. The nature of the job has been transformed by information technology. You should also be aware of predictions for office information systems and management techniques that will further alter administrative careers. The way you perform duties will continue to change, and technology will be your tool.

An IAAP survey of administrative professionals indicates the following results from respondents who were asked about technology use on the job.

Technological Tools Provided by Employer

Networked PC	95%
Color printer	85%
Scanner	69%
Access to work e-mail from home	61%
CD burner	60%
Teleconferencing system	48%
Digital copier	47%
Digital camera	42%
Laptop computer	35%
Videoconferencing system	34%

Wireless Internet access	28%
Cell phone	15%
PDA/handheld computer	12%
Voice recognition software	5%

Expanding Role of Administrative Assistants

The role of administrative assistants continues to grow mainly because they are in the right office technology environment at the right time. As the technology was introduced into the office, secretaries had to learn how to handle the equipment and software programs being used. They developed more sophisticated skills to process information. Then as downsizing was occurring, secretaries began assuming managerial responsibilities and emerged with more challenging jobs. In a 2005 poll of members of the IAAP, 78 percent of the respondents stated that their responsibilities increased in the past five years. The areas in which responsibilities grew are given in the list below. They are ranked on a scale of 0 to 10: 10 being the area of greatest increase in responsibilities, 0 being the area of least increase in responsibilities.[3]

Areas of Growth

General office management/information coordination/supervision	6.5
Travel planning	6.0

---

3. "Areas of job responsibilities that have increased most over past five years," International Association of Administrative Professionals, http://www.iaaphq.org/researchtrends/2005_iaap_profile_of_administrative_professionals_survey_results-2.htm, July 16, 2006.

Meeting planning 5.9
Project management (more long-term
projects) 5.8
Main liaison to corporate manager/
vice president 5.7
Online purchasing 5.4
Software training/troubleshooting 5.2
Storage and retrieval of information
(both paper and electronic formats) 5.0
Desktop publishing 4.2
Software adaptor (adapting software
to company needs) 3.8
Negotiator (with clients and vendors) 3.7
Team leader dealing with off-site
coworkers and traveling executives 3.6
Website design or content management 2.3

The explosion of office technology has definitely changed the way in which many office tasks are performed, who does the work, and what kinds of work are done. Computers have been the major thrust for these changes and have evolved into global communication tools as well as an integral part of business.

New procedures for workflow and completion of tasks are created and constantly revised. Goals are set, productivity is logged in and out, production is measured, formats are standardized, and administrative assistants are accountable. The administrative staff who work in an automated environment must understand the pattern of workflow so that they can understand relationships. Experts state that automation doesn't occur unless every person at every level, every thing, and every piece of equipment is integrated.

The phrase "just a secretary"—an individual who types correspondence and reports, who handles the telephone and clients, and who files and maintains a daily calendar—is a misnomer today. As you have seen, the use of automated equipment is changing the distribution of work in many offices. In some cases, traditional secretarial duties such as keyboarding, filing, photocopying, and bookkeeping are being assigned to workers in other units or departments. Professionals and managers increasingly do their own word processing and data entry and handle much of their own correspondence, rather than submit the work to secretaries and other support staff. Also, in some law and medical offices, paralegals and medical assistants are assuming some tasks formerly done by secretaries. As other workers assume more of these duties, there is a trend in many offices for professionals and managers to replace the traditional arrangement of one secretary per manager with administrative assistants who support the work of systems, departments, or units. This approach often means that administrative assistants assume added responsibilities and are seen as valuable members of a team.

Administrative assistants have an expanded role in the modern office as information managers. Their responsibilities can run from scheduling staff appointments to office management to managing an entire database. In today's world of work, this is a profession that not only calls for the execution of a wide range of specialized tasks but is also combined with changes in business technology.

Today's administrative assistants, a designation for the wide field that includes secretaries, are defined by the IAAP as "individuals who are responsible for administrative tasks and coordination of information in support of an office related environment and who are dedicated to furthering their personal and professional growth in their chosen profession."[4] The skills required to carry out this definition are organization, interpersonal communications, computer applications, negotiation, and time management. The role of the administrative assistant focuses on three growth areas:

1. **Computer software experts who play a central role in processing and distributing information.** A survey conducted by the IAAP indicates the extent to which administrative assistants use software. As expected, the greatest usage of computers is for word processing and e-mail, which are both 99 percent. (The list below provides the results of the survey.)

2. **Project managers who have been moving from short-term clerical tasks to multitask projects that involve greater responsibilities.** A large number of staff, 92 percent, now compose correspondence for both themselves and their managers.

3. **Supervisors and trainers who also represent their departments at meetings.** Formerly the purview of nonsecretarial personnel, today's administrative assistants are considered valuable contributors to inter- and intradepartmental meetings.

Usage of Software by Administrative Assistants

Word processing	99%
E-mail	99%
Spreadsheets	95%
Scheduling/calendaring	88%
Presentation	62%

---

4. International Association of Administrative Professionals. "Definition of Administrative Professional." International Association of Administrative Professionals, http://www.iaaphq.org/about.htm, July 13, 2006.

Database management	59%
Desktop publishing	39%
Accounting	29%
Project management	17%
Web design	14%
Authoring	8%
Voice recognition	5%

If you are interested in a career as an administrative assistant, you must accept the fact that change is constant in automated offices and that all levels of personnel are affected. For example, more and more executives can be seen using the computer for inputting as well as for decision making. Yes, you need to be computer literate to be able to operate equipment and use a variety of software packages; but more important are your knowledge of how computers work, your ability to analyze and solve a problem, your understanding of the ways in which new technology can be used, and your willingness to continue to learn and to adapt to changes.

4

Demand for
Administrative Assistants

Jobs that were once considered solid careers have now declined due to societal, global, and scientific forces that have led to the creation of new positions. According to the Bureau of Labor Statistics, total employment between now and 2014 will grow more slowly than it has in the past. This is because of changing methods in the way in which production and services are provided, such as changes in business technology. Most of the projected employment increase is in the services division of both business and health industries and in the service-production sector of the economy. An example of an employment decline in the administrative field would be for that of typists and word processors resulting from the growing use of word-processing equipment that increases efficiency and encourages office personnel to do more of the work themselves.

Secretarial and clerical work will continue to employ the largest number of workers, even though employment will grow at a slower than average pace. This occurs because of the large number of employees required in the field and the high turnover rate. There should also be opportunities for full-time and part-time work.

Although many have viewed the explosion of office technology as a threat to job security, the reverse is true. Office employment has been dramatically altered in number, type, responsibility, and nature of jobs available. The introduction of new services, as well as new products, has led to the creation of new kinds of jobs. Even though office automation increased productivity, this productivity has been offset by administrative assistants assuming responsibilities that were previously in the domain of managers and other professionals. In addition to this, soft skills such as flexibility, a positive personality, and a self-starter quality; use of discretion and diplomacy; and ability to be a team player are requirements employers want employees to possess.

If you wish to find work overseas, don't become overly optimistic because such jobs are not as plentiful or as attainable. The best approach to finding such a job is to become employed by the corporate headquarters of an international firm in the United States and then work toward this goal. You should also be aware that some countries place limitations on number and types of jobs that foreigners can fill and that the wages earned are frequently lower than comparable jobs in the United States.

Employment Statistics

In 2004 more than 4.1 million administrative assistants and secretaries were employed in the United States, compared with 3.4 million in 1997. In Canada, a total of 476,200 administrative assistants were employed, including 365,670 secretaries, 26,390 executive assistants, and 84,140 clerical supervisors.

Knowing the future projections of a particular career field is important so that you can make a wise decision. You will have certain preferences about environments in which you would like to work; therefore, examining job opportunities from an industry perspective is desirable. Following is a description of four major services industries: health services, advertising and public relations services, employment services, and social services. The data presented in Tables 4.1, 4.2, 4.3, and 4.4 will give you some comparison of the employment and percent change expected by 2014 in several types of industries.

Health Services

This is the largest industry in the country, with more than thirteen million jobs. Employment opportunities in the health services sector are expected to be excellent through 2014, with more than three million new jobs added to the economy during the projection period. Offices for physicians or dentists account for two-thirds of all private health service establishments. The bulk of the jobs in offices and clinics of physicians are in administrative support occupations, such as receptionists and medical secretaries, which make up two-fifths of the workers in physicians' offices. However, hospitals employ the largest percentage of workers. As an administrative assistant, you should become familiar with several health specialties to determine if any are of interest to you.

Table 4.1 shows that 2,379,000 administrative personnel were employed in this industry in 2004 and indicates a 16.2 percent growth of this occupation by 2014. Medical secretaries show that

Table 4.1 Health Services, 2004–2014 (Numbers in Thousands)

Occupation	Employment, 2004 Number	Percent	2004–2014 Percent Change
Office and Administrative Support Occupations	2,379	18.2	16.2
Billing and Posting Clerks and Machine Operators	179	1.4	10.9
Receptionists and Information Clerks	353	2.7	31.3
Medical Secretaries	347	2.7	17.3

Source: U.S. Department of Labor, Career Guide to Industries, Health Care, http://www.bls.gov/oco/cg/cgs035.htm#emply, July 26, 2006.

347,000 workers are employed with a 17.3 percent growth rate expected between 2004 and 2014.

Advertising and Public Relations Services

The goals of advertising and public relations services are to achieve favorable public exposure for clients and to develop strategies for them to obtain a certain public image. The administrative support occupations account for nearly 28 percent of employment in this field. Table 4.2 shows that 118,000 administrative assistants were employed in this industry in 2004 and indicates an 8.3 percent growth for this occupation by 2014.

Employment Services

This industry consists of employment agencies and helps supply services. Employment services companies provide temporary help to other businesses to supplement their workforce in special situations, such as during employee absences or increased seasonal work-

Table 4.2 Advertising and Public Relations Services, 2004–2014 (Numbers in Thousands)

Occupation	Employment, 2004 Number	Percent	2004–2014 Percent Change
Office and Administrative Support Occupations	118	27.8	8.3
First-Line Supervisors/Managers of Office and Administrative Support Workers	8	1.8	15.2
Bookkeeping, Accounting, and Auditing Clerks	11	2.6	14.4
Customer Service Representatives	14	3.3	30.1
Receptionists and Information Clerks	5	1.2	21.1
Secretaries and Administrative Assistants	18	4.3	14.9
Office Clerks, General	13	3.1	13.1

Source: U.S. Department of Labor, Career Guide to Industries, http://www.bls.gov/oco/cg/cgs030.htm#emply, July 26, 2006.

load. The employment services firm contracts temporary workers to a "client" at a specified fee. Many companies are especially receptive to hiring these temps even full-time rather than employing permanent staff members, which require significantly greater employee benefits. This industry encompasses a wide range of fields from administrative support occupations such as administrative assistants to professional occupations such as nurse. Administrative assistants are needed in every phase of business, including banks, insurance companies, investment and real estate firms, law firms, educational institutions, as well as in federal, state, and local government agencies. Employment services is one of the fastest-growing industries and one that is expected to provide the most new jobs, which are expected to grow 43 percent over the 2004–2014 period. This is almost four times the 14 percent growth anticipated for all industries combined. Table 4.3 shows that 848,000 administrative assistants were employed in 2004 and indicates a 43 percent growth for this occupation by 2014.

Social Services

This industry usually appeals to individuals who are interested in helping others. The need exists in this industry, as in many others, for administrative support workers as well as managers. Generally, earnings of nonsupervisory personnel are below the average for all private industry. Table 4.4 shows that 170,000 administrative assistants were employed in 2004 and indicates a 17.9 percent growth for this occupation by 2014.

Table 4.3 Employment Services, 2004–2014 (Numbers in Thousands)

Occupation	Employment, 2004 Number	Percent	2004–2014 Percent Change
Office and Administrative Support Occupations	848	24.4	43.0
Bookkeeping, Accounting, and Auditing Clerks	39	1.1	47.0
Customer Service Representatives	79	2.3	74.4
File Clerks	27	0.8	−18.3
Receptionists and Information Clerks	61	1.8	55.6
Secretaries and Administrative Assistants	133	3.8	41.0
Data-Entry Keyers	51	1.5	30.7
Word Processors and Typists	21	0.6	11.2
Office Clerks, General	182	5.2	49.3

Source: U.S. Department of Labor, Career Guide to Industries,http://www.bls.gov/oco/cg/ cgs039.htm#emply, July 26, 2006.

Administrative Assistant Occupations in Canada

Similar to the United States, the fastest-growing sector in Canada's economy is the service sector, thus accounting for the largest increase in jobs. Approximately two-thirds of all Canadians are employed in this category. The data and information that follow about clerical occupations/general office skills (includes administrative and office assistants); secretaries, recorders, and transcriptionists; medical secretaries; and legal secretaries present an overview of the field. This is a predominantly female occupation.

- **Clerical occupations/general office skills.** These employees work both for the government and the private sector. Approximately 52 percent are general office clerks and 32 percent are receptionists. Of this total, 21 percent work part-time, which is slightly higher than the average for all occupations. Women account

Table 4.4 Social Services, 2004–2014 (Numbers in Thousands)

| Occupation | Employment, 2004 | | 2004–2014 |
	Number	Percent	Percent Change
Office and Administrative			
Support Occupations	170	12.4	17.9
Supervisors, Office and			
Administrative Support Workers	12	0.9	20.2
Bookkeeping, Accounting, and			
Auditing Clerks	17	1.3	19.5
Receptionists and Information			
Clerks	17	1.3	26.5
Secretaries and Administrative			
Assistants	45	3.3	18.8
Office Clerks, General	37	2.7	18.1

Source: U.S. Department of Labor, Career Guide to Industries, http://www.bls.gov/oco/cg/cgs040.htm#emply, July 27, 2006.

for 82 percent of clerical workers. Employment is moderately sensitive to business conditions, and technological advances may have a negative effect on the group due to the increasing use of computers, facsimile equipment, electronic mail, and related software. The majority of clerical staff employed in the private sector work in finance, insurance, and real estate.

• **Secretaries, recorders, and transcriptionists.** These employees work in government and throughout the private sector including law offices, real estate companies, hospitals and doctors' offices, and other types of organizations. This group includes specialized secretaries such as technical, medical, legal, estate, and litigation secretaries as well as court reporters and stenographers.

Of this group, 631,000 were employed in 2004, which is 5 percent of the workforce. Secretaries account for 80 percent of the group, and women make up 92 percent of all these workers.

• **Medical secretaries.** These employees work in doctors' offices, hospitals, clinics, and other medical settings. Of this group, 58 percent work for physicians, health practitioners, and medical labs, followed by 38 percent who work in hospitals. In 2004, 42,000 were employed as medical secretaries. About 24 percent work part-time, well above the average for all occupations. In this specialty, 99 percent are women. It is interesting to note that private health care practices continue to be the center for job creation in this occupation.

• **Legal secretaries.** These employees work in government, law offices, land title offices, and in courts at the municipal, provincial, and federal levels. In this group, the large majority work in professional offices—81 percent. The number of legal secretaries who were employed in this profession in 2004 was 42,000, a growth rate of 4 percent more than in 1994. Part-timers account for 12 percent of the employees. In this specialty, too, 99 percent are women. It should be noted that most of the employment growth for legal secretaries is projected to be in private law practices.

Male-Female Employment in Administrative Careers

The secretarial field is one of the largest, and it has historically been dominated by women. With the changes occurring throughout the workforce, there appears to be a blurring of the traditional demarcation between jobs for men and women in many occupations. Does this apply to administrative assistants as well? More men are enrolling in office administration curricula, which might be the result of variations in department names to reflect the nature of the field and changing responsibilities of administrative personnel. Some new titles are: department of office technology, office and systems administration, and department of secretarial and office information systems.

Some comments from men who work as administrative assistants reveal the following reasons for pursuing this field: "Serving others and being at the top of things and networking with counterparts are only a few of the rewards achieved from this career." "Successful secretaries have adapted to the information age by expanding their job skills. They realized long ago that knowledge is power." "The profession was intriguing to me since very few males sought entrance, and I wanted to secure a future with skills that would be helpful in landing a job." Other reasons for men entering the field include nationwide opportunities in a variety of industries, involvement with high technology, and challenging responsibilities. While men are gradually becoming attracted to this career because of the changing work environment and the diverse opportunities that exist, as Table 4.5 indicates, administrative occupations are still predominantly staffed by women.

Salaries and Benefits

The changing times, increasing office automation, and innovative business practices all have had some effect on the work environment for administrative assistants, but they have not resulted in a lack of demand for qualified personnel. Job openings should be plentiful for those who are qualified and experienced, primarily due to replacement of those who transfer to other occupations or leave for other reasons.

Salaries for administrative assistants vary greatly, reflecting differences in level of skill, experience, and responsibility. In addition, salaries in different parts of the country vary depending on demand, current salary scales of industry, and availability of personnel. Generally, compensation in large cities is higher than in small towns, and the earnings on the East and West Coasts are above the earnings in the Midwest or South. Those cities that offer the highest salaries are New York, Boston, and Los Angeles with Washington, DC, and San Francisco close behind. Also, salaries of administrative assistants tend to be highest in transportation, legal services, and public utilities. Certification in the field is generally recognized by an increase in salary. It is significant that salaries for these administrative personnel reach a high point that exceeds those of all other clerical positions.

You will also want to bear in mind that salary differentials may reflect the increased cost of living in a given area. Investigate the

Table 4.5 Percent of Female Administrative Professionals (Numbers in Thousands)

Occupation	Total Employed	Percent Women
Administrative Support Occupations, Including Clerical	18,184	78.0
Supervisors: Administrative Support	717	60.5
Supervisors: General Office	402	69.4
Supervisors: Financial Records Processing	107	81.6
Supervisors: and Distribution, Scheduling, and Adjusting Clerks	185	31.6
Computer Equipment Operators	308	47.1
Computer Operators	301	46.9
Secretaries, Stenographers, and Typists	3,020	97.6
Secretaries	2,302	98.6
Stenographers	146	95.2
Typists	571	93.9
Information Clerks	2,053	89.0
Interviewers	169	82.2
Hotel Clerks	131	70.1
Transportation Ticket and Reservation Agents	237	72.7
Receptionists	1,068	97.1
Miscellaneous Administrative Support Occupations	3,858	84.2
General Office Clerks	842	83.3
Bank Tellers	477	87.3
Data-Entry Keyers	595	81.8
Statistical Clerks	97	85.1
Teachers' Aides	813	91.6
Records Processing, Except Financial	995	80.5
Order Clerks	289	74.9
Personnel Clerks	70	79.1
Library Clerks	130	79.2
File Clerks	288	81.5
Records Clerks	206	87.4

Source: U.S. Department of Labor, Current Population Survey, http://www.bls.gov/cps/wlf tables11.pdf, July 27, 2006.

fixed expenses of rent, taxes, and other significant items that may be higher than the area in which you presently live before you consider a move. A list of the expenses where you live can be used as a starting point. You can request information from the chamber of commerce where you are thinking of moving, from friends, and from such organizations as church groups, civic organizations, schools, and banks.

U.S. Salaries

The figures in Table 4.6 were compiled by the OfficeTeam researchers. They reflect starting salary information in the various areas of administrative work.

You will also be interested in glancing at the median annual salaries in the different parts of the country, as illustrated in Table 4.7. This might be a factor to consider when you look for a job.

If you wish to relocate, notice for example the difference in salary between the East and the West Coasts. Whereas the average annual income for office managers in the Northeast is $61,253, in the Southwest it is nearly ten thousand dollars less.

Canadian Salaries

The wide range of salaries in Canada, shown in Table 4.8 (page 57), depends on region, skill, experience, and responsibilities of the position. Salary figures given in the table are in Canadian dollars.

Benefits

Although benefits are considered apart from salaries, they nevertheless have a substantial monetary value that you should carefully consider. Think about the cost of hospitalization, medical insur-

Table 4.6 U.S. Salary Ranges 2006–2007

Title	2006	2007	% Change
Senior Executive Assistant	$37,000–$51,200	$39,000–$54,750	6.5
Executive Assistant	$32,000–$42,000	$34,000–$44,750	6.4
Senior Administrative Assistant	$29,000–$36,000	$30,000–$39,000	6.2
Administrative Assistant	$26,000–$31,750	$26,250–$34,000	4.3
Entry-Level Administrative Assistant	$21,500–$27,750	$23,000–$28,500	4.6
Senior Office/Facilities Manager	$36,500–$46,250	$37,500–$52,000	8.2
Office/Facilities Manager	$31,250–$38,000	$32,500–$42,000	7.6
Human Resources Assistant	$25,750–$34,000	$26,500–$35,000	2.9
Marketing Assistant	$26,500–$33,000	$26,750–$34,000	2.1
Sales Assistant	$26,000–$32,250	$26,250–$34,000	3.4
Medical Executive Assistant	$31,250–$40,750	$33,000–$43,000	5.6
Front Desk Coordinator	$21,250–$27,000	$22,000–$28,250	3.6
Receptionist	$20,000–$25,500	$21,000–$26,750	4.9
Senior Customer Service/ Call Center Rep	$25,750–$36,500	$26,500–$38,000	3.6
Customer Service/ Call Center Rep	$20,750–$28,000	$21,500–$29,000	3.6
Medical Office Administrator	$36,250–$48,000	$36,500–$48,250	0.6
Project Coordinator	$28,750–$37,750	$29,250–$39,000	2.6
Presentation/Graphics Specialist	$31,250–$41,500	$32,000–$43,000	3.1
Logistics Coordinator	$28,250–$35,250	$28,750–$37,000	3.5

The above figures are projections for starting salaries. Bonuses, incentives, and other forms of compensation such as benefits and retirement packages are not reflected.

Source: OfficeTeam 2007 Salary Guide, www.officeteam.com.

ance, vacation benefits, life insurance, and retirement plans, for example. The preestablished benefits that were provided are now being replaced in some companies by pick-and-choose plans or *cafeteria plans,* as they are frequently called. Other companies now

Table 4.7 Median Annual Salaries in Selected U.S. Metropolitan Areas

Job Title	Northeast	Northwest	Southeast	Southwest	Midwest
Administrative Assistant I	$42,558	$39,627	$36,115	$35,942	$38,834
Administrative Services Supervisor	$64,544	$60,100	$54,773	$54,511	$58,896
Document Control Clerk	$38,822	$36,148	$32,945	$32,787	$35,425
Executive Assistant	$51,867	$48,295	$44,015	$43,804	$47,328
IT Generalist	$57,516	$53,556	$48,809	$48,576	$52,483
Legal Secretary II	$42,094	$39,195	$35,721	$35,550	$38,410
Office Automation Analyst	$62,764	$58,442	$53,263	$53,008	$57,272
Office Manager	$61,253	$57,035	$51,980	$51,731	$55,893
Secretary II	$40,287	$37,513	$34,188	$34,024	$36,762
Secretary to CEO	$70,481	$65,628	$59,811	$59,525	$64,314
Word Processing Operator	$39,834	$37,091	$33,803	$33,642	$36,348

Source: U.S. Department of Labor, 2006 National Summary of Occupational Compensation Survey, www.bls.gov/ocs.

require employees to pay for a portion of their health coverage. Plans will vary as employers adopt them. For example, a firm might give its employees a core of basic benefits, such as those mentioned above; then from another group of options, employees may select benefits up to a maximum amount.

Do not expect all kinds of benefits. Companies are trying to find ways to cut the costs of providing benefits. Be sure you know what your benefits will be when you accept a job.

Table 4.8 Median Annual Salaries in Selected Canadian Provinces

Job Title	Alberta	British Columbia	Nova Scotia	Ontario	Quebec
Administrative Assistant	$38,764	$41,514	$35,409	$41,846	$40,136
Administrative Services Manager	$61,198	$65,539	$55,902	$66,063	$63,364
Data Entry Clerk II	$30,439	$32,598	$27,805	$32,859	$31,516
Executive Secretary	$40,880	$43,780	$37,342	$44,130	$42,327
Human Resources Assistant	$39,342	$42,133	$35,938	$42,470	$40,735
Office Manager	$53,017	$56,778	$48,429	$57,232	$54,894
Secretary II	$35,635	$38,163	$32,551	$38,468	$36,896
Secretary Corporate	$113,638	$121,700	$103,805	$122,673	$117,660
Word Processing Operator	$34,030	$36,445	$31,086	$36,763	$35,235

Source: Salary Wizard Canada,http://swz.salary.com/csalarywizard/layoutscripts/cswzl_new
search.asp, July 23, 2006.

The Wage Gap

In evaluation studies of a job, the factors measured are the inherent skills of the job, effort needed to perform the job, responsibility, and working conditions. Traditionally, women have performed clerical work. Although women have been fighting for equality and some progress has been made, a gap still exists between women's and men's earnings.

According to Women Employed, a leading national advocate for women's economic advancement, although 62 percent of working women earn half or more of their family's income, and 77 percent of all mothers with school-age children work, women earn only 77 cents for every dollar earned by men. In addition, female high school graduates earn 34 percent less than male high school graduates, and female college graduates earn 33 percent less than their male counterparts.[1]

If you experience problems with equal pay for equal work, visit the Equal Employment Opportunity Commission website at www.eeoc.gov for information about what to do.

In the office support occupations in Canada, more than 95 percent of the employees are women, with the exception of clerical occupations/general office skills, where 82 percent of the workers are women. According to Statistics Canada, the wage gap is similar to that in the United States. Statistics indicate that earnings of women are lower than the average level in practically all of the office occupations.

The Alternative Workplace

The traditional office environment is no longer the sole focus of the workplace. Alternative workplaces that incorporate nontraditional locations and practices supplement the usual office, moving the work to the worker. What precipitated this movement? As you have seen, women account for a large percentage of the labor force. They are now interested in lifelong careers and frequently are multiple jobholders. What do these changes in lifestyles, values, and social patterns mean in terms of employment? First, firms want to retain their valuable employees. Women need to balance their work and

---

1. Women Employed, http://www.womenemployed.org/index.php?id=20, July 30, 2006.

home life; therefore, it is necessary to adopt innovative work patterns that are flexible in work schedules and locations. Second, since women have the needed skills and productive capacity to help support the country's economic growth, business has to respond to their needs by establishing alternative work patterns that would spur recruitment, improve morale, and reduce absenteeism and turnover.

Another important reason for developing alternative work patterns is to reduce the amount of space utilized and lower overhead costs. Many large corporations have greatly reduced their costs by eliminating offices that people don't need, consolidating others, and reducing related overhead costs. This section will explore how and where work can be done and the many forms an alternative workplace can take.

Part-Time Work

Part-time workers make up a large group of employees. Generally, these workers are students, young people not ready for full-time commitments, mothers who need the extra income but only want to work while their young children are in school, or mature individuals with family responsibilities. Part-time employment means working fewer than thirty-five hours a week; however, the usual time frame is to work three days a week or twenty hours per week.

Today, part-time employment is used in different ways, according to the Department of Labor. Some workers combine several part-time jobs to make up a full workweek. Others hold a full-time primary job and a part-time secondary job. Approximately ten million workers hold more than one job at a time, and more than half of all moonlighters in 2004 combined a full-time job with a part-time job. In the administrative support profession, approximately 8.5 percent of those employed were multiple jobholders.

Opportunities for employment in administrative assistant positions as part-timers continue to increase as employers see the benefits in reduced labor costs and flexibility in hiring staff when needed. Kelly Services of Troy, Michigan, and Manpower Inc. of Milwaukee, Wisconsin, two of the largest sources of part-timer employees, report that the need for part-timer employees has grown so fast that they cannot readily fill temporary job openings.

Compressed Workweek

Some businesses allow employees to use an alternative schedule. Instead of working a full five-day week schedule, a popular option is to compress the forty hours into a four-day week. Another choice is to work twelve hours a day for three days. This type of scheduling allows for extended hours for the company and a weekday for employees to use for personal responsibilities.

Flextime

Flextime, a concept in scheduling daily work hours for full-time employees, is receiving favorable acceptance in many companies and continues to be adopted throughout the country. There are variations of flextime scheduling; however, personnel usually work during a core period each day. From options established by management, workers select the time that completes a day's productivity. For example, employees might have the choice of arriving at work between 6:30 and 10:00 A.M. and leaving between 3:00 and 6:30 P.M. Thus, employees have some control over their workday. Occasionally, a company will offer a four-day workweek that narrows down to a ten-hour day.

Flextime has resulted in positive effects on employee attitudes, and sick leave is less abused. A recent business survey indicated that more firms are adopting flextime scheduling. They claim it increases efficiency and morale and decreases absenteeism and turnover. One can assume from this finding that as personnel satisfaction increases, company image is improved. This gives a firm a competitive advantage in the marketplace. Productivity usually is maintained or increased, and many employee benefits are realized. Although flextime was originally designed for lower-level employees, some Fortune 500 organizations are now extending this work pattern to managers and professional employees.

Telecommuting

Telecommuting is one of the most recognized forms of alternative workplaces. Because work is performed electronically wherever the employee is, telecommuting frequently supplements the traditional office rather than replacing it.

Telecommuting initially involved employees working at home or at a satellite office on a computer or terminal and communicating by phone to the home office. This concept has been broadened and includes those individuals who work out of a customer's office or who communicate with the office via laptop or mobile telephone. Interestingly, Alvin Toffler in his 1980 book *The Third Wave* predicted that millions of Americans would establish automated work centers in their homes. His predictions became a reality as computers, fax machines, and modems became accessible in terms of pricing, and America grew into an information-based society.

Companies vary widely in the approaches they use with home offices. Some allow employees to use their own discretion. Others provide laptops, dedicated phone lines, software support, fax-printer units, help lines, and full technical backup at the nearest corporate facility.

One health-related facility implemented a telecommuting program because it became increasingly difficult to find qualified medical secretaries. Management worked out a program whereby physicians dictated over the telephone to a central system, secretaries accessed the information through telephone lines, and the documents were transcribed on computers. At a scheduled time each evening, the day's work was transmitted through communication lines back to the clinic where it was printed.

Of course, there are many concerns about whether telecommuting will really work in the long run because employees cannot develop a sense of belonging that fulfills psychological needs, nor can they be part of the informal interaction in the office. Another disadvantage is the inability of the telecommuter to be a team player because a home-based work environment doesn't permit him or her to have that kind of interactive work experience. Also, communication via e-mail is not a substitute for personal interaction.

If you will be telecommuting, follow these tips for success.

- Plan your working hours without interruptions.
- Design an organized working environment.
- Maintain a work agenda for you and your manager to review.
- Plan regular meetings at the office with your supervisor or manager.
- Become part of a team or group and attend regular meetings at the office.
- Communicate by e-mail or in writing on progress of work at the beginning of each week.

- Keep your workplace at home private.
- Share your home office with your coworkers for meetings.
- Network with other telecommuters and staff.

Job Sharing

Another alternative to full-time employment is job sharing, where two people assume responsibilities for one job. They divide the work between them and arrange their own schedules to provide full-time coverage on the job. Job sharing differs from part-time work in which an individual is an independent employee who has the sole responsibility for a particular job.

Advocates of nontraditional work groups point out several advantages of job sharing.

- Job sharers are interested in careers and advancement.
- Productivity will probably increase because of greater job satisfaction, more concentrated effort, and lower rates of absenteeism and turnover.
- Coverage can be arranged during peak periods or absenteeism due to sickness.
- Greater continuity occurs in job performance. If one of the job sharers leaves the job, the partner can usually fill in while a new person is being trained.

Unless carefully planned, job sharing can fail. Some factors companies consider are recognition of each individual's strengths and weaknesses, parity with full-time positions in terms of salaries and benefits, clearly understood expectations, and voluntary job sharing. Personnel factors to be taken into account when establishing such a working arrangement are good communication skills, organizational ability, cooperativeness, and similarity of work values.

Although many employers have expressed resistance to such programs, others endorse the concept and have initiated it.

Temporary Employment

The traditional idea of hiring a temporary employee to fill in for a receptionist who is sick or on vacation has changed radically in the past few years. Temporary help performing all sorts of work is used throughout the company. This type of hiring falls into the category of contract staffing in which the temporary employee is obtained from a help supply service firm that is the employer of this individual. Much of this practice is due to global competition and downsizing. Advantages for the employer include having available staff without the burden of paying for benefits, fewer layoffs in slow seasons, decrease in record keeping, replacement of unsatisfactory workers, and screening of employees for qualifications and experience. The benefits for the temporary worker are experience in different types of organizations, development of skills, and a growing list of references.

Two other trends in staffing the office are outsourcing and employee leasing. Outsourcing is a form of contract staffing that transfers business functions to a third party. Smaller companies frequently use outsourcing because they can't justify a full-time, experienced employee on staff, or perhaps they have difficulty hiring and retaining such experts. Outsourcing may also be used to augment the manpower already on the payroll. Some midsize organizations are resorting to selective outsourcing where they off-load only one or two tasks.

In leasing, a long-term permanent arrangement, the customer has a contractual agreement with the leasing firm, which is the employer. The advantage of these two trends is that the customer never handles payroll, taxes, insurance benefits, vacations, or other administrative items.

If you are looking for challenge and excitement and want to become acquainted with different kinds of companies, temporary employment might be an approach you should investigate. Each day is different, for you never know what you are getting into. One basic advantage of working as a temp is the opportunity of determining whether you like the job and its environment. This might also lead to a permanent job if you have the right skills and attitude. While you are working as a temp, take advantage of the training most temporary staffing agencies offer to make you more marketable.

5

TYPES OF
ADMINISTRATIVE ASSISTANTS

No MATTER WHETHER it is a multinational firm or small business, secretarial and administrative support work evolves around new office automation and company restructuring. New strategies based on controlling costs and improving productivity are changing the way business is done, which affects administrative workers. Generally, their roles and responsibilities have expanded. The workload is increasing, tasks are more varied, and they are assuming management duties and obligations. Administrative assistants and secretaries basically manage information. Their responsibilities run the gamut from producing correspondence and reports to scheduling staff appointments to office management to managing an entire database. Few professions require such skillful knowledge and ability to execute so many specialized tasks.

Administrative support personnel need to have a broad set of skills that include processing documents, distributing information, managing records and files, organizing and planning, maintaining equipment and supplies, and performing specific financial functions. Increasingly, administrative assistants are producing spreadsheets and databases as well as using desktop publishing and graphics programs. Clearly these qualifications show the need to be computer literate and technology oriented in order to be successful. Administrative personnel must learn to think like managers. With this change comes more empowerment and freedom in jobs as well as responsibility.

Chapter 3 discussed the variety of titles that are currently used for administrative personnel. The following terms can be added to that list: *specialized secretary, senior secretary/assistant, transcription specialist, administrative receptionist,* and *word processing/administrative assistant.* These designations frequently don't reflect the qualifications, duties, and responsibilities of the various positions. As mentioned previously, few other professionals have to be capable of performing such a variety of tasks and projects. Jobs vary and require different skills for the nature of the position. When searching for a job, look under the various titles. Read the ads carefully and be prepared to ask questions about the job to determine if it will be a good experience with potential for you.

There is a constant need for secretaries and administrative assistants in many industries, whether in traditional business offices, automated environments, or offices of specialists. Since this is one of the largest employment fields, there is a constant need for new employees. Also, many secretarial duties are of an interactive nature and are not easily automated. For example, planning conferences, working with clients, and dealing with staff require tact and diplomacy in addition to communication skills. Automated equipment cannot substitute for these personal skills; therefore, secretaries will continue to play an important role in most organizations. In addition to the general, behavioral, and technical administrative skills, employers may seek individuals who have specialized training or experience in technical, legal, or medical areas.

This chapter will introduce you to the many professional administrative career specializations to help you choose the career best suited to your own interests and talents.

Levels of Administrative Personnel

In the traditional office, administrative assistants and secretaries generally work on a one-to-one relationship with the principal. However, that is atypical today, as secretaries usually are assigned to several individuals. The senior partner may still be supported by the traditional secretary, who functions as a generalist, performs diverse tasks, uses a computer for document production, and is knowledgeable about office routines and procedures as well as the organization. Responsibilities of the general secretary, no matter what the title is, might include duties extending into personnel administration, supervision, management, and other areas.

The National Compensation Survey, published by the U.S. Department of Labor, lists ten criteria that are used to determine the levels or ranking of an occupation based on the requirements of the position. These factors are taken from the U.S. Government Office of Personnel Management's Factor Evaluation System:

1. Knowledge
2. Supervision received
3. Guidelines (for example, judgment needed to apply procedures and policies, use of reference manuals, and so forth)

4. Complexity (number, variety, and intricacy of tasks and methods in work performed)
5. Scope and effect (depth of assignment and effect on others)
6. Personal contact
7. Purpose of contacts
8. Physical demands
9. Work environment
10. Supervisory duties

The Bureau of Labor Statistics develops data on five levels of secretaries and administrative assistants. Level one is the entry level, where an employee performs duties under specific instructions of a supervisor and handles a general range of office duties including inputting on a computer, transcribing dictation, and performing other office functions. At level two the secretary works under the supervisor's general instructions, and at level three he or she exercises judgment and initiative in handling nonroutine situations and works with the approval of the supervisor on other situations. By level four the employee is handling independently a wide variety of situations and conflicts involving clerical or administrative functions of the office. Level five is the highest level of achievement and has a significant number of managerial responsibilities.

Administrative assistants in traditional offices are generalists or individuals who perform all support functions. They are basically information workers who process and transmit information within and outside the organization. They must possess certain intangible qualities that are not easily measured to carry out the duties of the position. For example, the worker must be able to make value judgments as to the importance of the following: incoming communications and telephone calls, items that require immediate responses, communications that he or she can answer, calls that should be transferred to other staff members, and documents that should be held for future reference.

Another important aspect of an administrative assistant's job is interaction with executives, managers, staff, clients, and suppliers. Are good human relations skills being used? Is the worker presenting a favorable image of the office and company?

Position Descriptions

As you read the job descriptions below, you will note that *secretary* and *administrative assistant* are titles used interchangeably for the same type of position. However, there are differences between the word processing and secretarial specializations. Word processing support staff handle the keyboarding tasks and document production for principals and other staff who either forward handwritten material or dictate directly to either the centralized or decentralized center where the tapes are transcribed. Secretaries and administrative assistants perform a wide range of duties such as screening calls, receiving and directing visitors, filing, scheduling meetings, editing, gathering information, and keeping digests of mail.

The job descriptions that follow are adapted from the 2004 Salary Guide put out by OfficeTeam, a specialized administrative staffing service.

• **Receptionist/Administrative Assistant.** Receives and routes telephone calls, greets visitors, handles filing, distributes mail, photocopies, faxes, provides administrative support at various levels within organization, and uses computers.

- **Administrative Assistant/Secretary I (up to three years of experience).** Performs administrative and office support activities for multiple supervisors; includes departmental secretaries. Duties may include fielding telephone calls, receiving and directing visitors, typing, word processing, filing, and faxing. Requires basic and intermediate computer expertise and strong communication skills.
- **Administrative Assistant/Secretary II (three or more years of experience).** Duties include those of Administrative Assistant/Secretary I; support senior-level managers; maintain high level of computer expertise with ability to train others in systems usage.
- **Executive Assistant/Executive Secretary I (up to four years of experience).** Performs administrative duties for senior management. Responsibilities may include screening calls, making travel and meeting arrangements, preparing reports and financial data, handling customer relations, and training and supervising other support staff. Requires intermediate-level computer skills, including proficiency with spreadsheet, presentation, and database applications; flexibility; excellent interpersonal and communication skills; project coordinator expertise; and the ability to interact with all levels of management.
- **Executive Assistant/Executive Secretary II (five or more years of experience).** Duties include those described for Executive Secretary I, advanced communication skills, and ability to train others on systems usage; ability to support the most senior management personnel, particularly in large corporations; and possibly supervision of other administrative staff.

Specialized Fields

Four administrative professional positions require specialized knowledge and abilities: legal, medical, technical, and educational.

Other options for those who want an interesting and varied career include running a private secretarial firm or becoming a stenographer or court reporter.

Legal

The role of the legal secretary has changed similarly to that of the general secretary. Legal secretaries need to be computer literate, understand the terminology, and have the specialized knowledge required in a legal environment. In the past, shorthand skills were a requirement; today these skills are looked upon very favorably in the higher-level positions and frequently are requested by senior partners. In some firms, legal secretaries conduct the research, schedule depositions, and answer clients' questions.

Legal secretaries prepare legal documents such as summonses, complaints, motions, petitions, subpoenas, answers, living trusts, deeds, affidavits, and briefs. They may also be in charge of the law library, adding parts and other material to update editions as the law and precedent change. In addition to the typical responsibilities of taking and transcribing dictation and performing administrative office functions required in any office, other duties include the following: reviewing law journals, assisting with legal research, taking notes on proceedings, maintaining corporate records, filing papers in the courthouse, taking notes, and maintaining the lawyer's files during a trial; investigating cases for trial and obtaining information that the lawyer must have to prepare certain documents; advising the lawyer of court appearances and due dates for filing pleadings; and maintaining escrow accounts.

In addition to having office skills and personal traits that are far above average, a successful legal secretary should be an expert at time management and juggling many activities and roles at the same time. Psychological skills in dealing daily with many different personalities and using excellent judgment to make dozens of critical decisions are also important characteristics.

Several factors in the legal services field will affect the future of the legal secretary. Clients expect more accountability for the fees they pay. In addition, the increase in the number of paralegal firms will increase employment opportunities. These firms offer lower rates than a traditional attorney's office for services such as preparing wills, uncontested divorces, and name changes.

No two jobs in the legal profession are alike, with marked differences between the duties of a legal secretary in a one- or two-lawyer office compared to a large firm employing many lawyers. A special code of conduct is required of legal secretaries, and this is spelled out in the code of ethics developed by the National Association of Legal Secretaries (NALS). Every member shall[1]:

- Encourage respect for the law and administration of justice
- Observe the rules governing privileged communications and confidential information
- Promote and exemplify high standards of loyalty, cooperation, and courtesy
- Perform all duties of the profession with integrity and competence
- Pursue a high order of professional attainment

Being a legal secretary is a highly respected position. Excellent office skills are necessary, and the qualities that enable you to work well with highly trained professionals are desirable as well.

---

1. NALS, http://www.nals.org/aboutnals/code/index.html, July 23, 2006.

Job opportunities are unlimited for legal secretaries, with choices of specialization in patent, criminal, real estate, malpractice, corporate, matrimonial, probate, or negligence law. In recent years, environmental law and public interest law have also emerged. There is a trend toward increasing specialization in large law firms that employ large numbers of legal secretaries.

If you are interested in diverse activities, the small, private law firm might be for you. It offers the widest variety of work and the greatest opportunity for individual initiative. Large law firms or legal departments of corporations usually provide well defined work. However, an advantage of working in corporate departments is that hours of employment are more regular; in law firms, no matter what size, frequently the legal secretary is called upon to work overtime.

Views from a Secretary and a Lawyer

Carol Ann Wilson is an experienced legal secretary. She takes a great deal of pride in her profession and is particularly proud of the knowledge and experience she has gained throughout her career. Wilson has worked on high-profile cases and met famous people, handling important responsibilities for her employers. Wilson says, "I have been trusted with information that is so confidential that, had I been working for the government, I would have had the highest security clearance."

Luther J. Avery of Bancroft, Avery, and McAlister in San Francisco believes there is a need for qualified legal secretaries who perform a vital role in the delivery of legal services. As changes have occurred in the legal profession and the delivery of legal services, some things have remained constant, such as the need for a strong personal and confidential relationship between lawyer and client;

the intellectual stimulation gained from problem solving and helping people; and the need for quality services and attention to detail.

Avery sees a growing need for competent legal secretaries and would not be surprised to see a shortage in the future. He feels that while the legal secretary may need more skills or education, this is part of the challenge that makes the job interesting. He believes that the competent legal secretary is and will continue to be an administrator, a facilitator, and the key person on the law office production line who will help maintain the quality of legal products and services.

The essential skills, knowledge, and attitudes of the legal secretary are spelled out in the literature of such organizations as the NALS. Where the lawyer-client relationship is dependent upon the integrity and intelligence of the participants and is responsive to personal problems, there is a continuing need for the professionalism, skills, knowledge, and attitudes exhibited by legal secretaries.

Without legal secretaries involved in the delivery of legal services, lawyers and the legal system would have difficulty functioning. If you are interested in employment as a legal secretary, try to obtain a broad education and learn management skills and computer skills as well as personnel relations, human relations, and technical skills. Most of all, in seeking employment as a legal secretary, be careful to select your employer wisely, because whether or not you will enjoy the legal secretarial profession will probably depend upon the environment in which you function.

Medical

According to the Department of Labor Statistics, professional specialty and service occupations in the health services industry cover nearly three out of five jobs. The next largest share of jobs is in administrative support occupations.

Over time, the health-care industry has experienced unprecedented growth. The proliferation of medical centers, family medicine clinics, extended health-care facilities, private group practices, and long-term-care facilities has created a need for administrative personnel who possess good office skills, knowledge of medical terminology, training in administrative and clinical procedures, and a "caring" attitude.

Administrative jobs and responsibilities in medical offices vary. For example, you might be responsible for business activities in the office, you might be the receptionist who greets patients when they walk into a doctor's office or hospital, or you might be an assistant who helps patients in preparing for examinations or for certain medical procedures, such as taking blood pressure and temperature. As a medical secretary, you will have many opportunities for challenges of this nature.

Whether you choose to work in a small doctor's office or in a large medical center, you will undoubtedly perform diverse duties every day. In addition to handling the general office routines, you may prepare papers for hospital admissions, obtain patient information, maintain the appointment book, prepare information for referrals, complete insurance forms, arrange for payment of fees, keep reminders for renewals of licenses and memberships in organizations, order supplies and drugs, transcribe and maintain records of the patients' medical histories, and deal with pharmaceutical representatives who visit the office to discuss new products with the doctor.

As you become more familiar with the medical secretarial career, you will realize that in addition to hospitals, clinics, and private doctors' offices, you could find employment with a medical research foundation, in companies that manufacture drugs, in health-related organizations such as Blue Cross/Blue Shield, and in the medical departments of large corporations that provide employees with health services.

In addition to promotional opportunities as a supervisor or manager, you may wish to become a medical assistant. In this position, you would continue to perform the typical secretarial and administrative tasks and would also perform certain clinical duties and procedures. The employment outlook for both types of medical secretarial careers is excellent.

You might also want to consider becoming a medical transcriptionist, which is another allied health career. Medical transcriptionists work with physicians, pharmacists, radiologists, nurses, and dieticians. These workers must know the language of medical and surgical specialties. They transcribe medical histories and data collected from physicals, operative reports, consultations, discharge summaries, and a long list of other subspecialty documentations. They need a command of medical terminology, very good keyboarding and editing skills, excellent auditory skills, and highly developed analytical skills. An individual who is interested in a career as a medical transcriptionist is assured of a flexible work schedule and an intellectually challenging position.

A Medical Secretary's Point of View

Janice Nicosia, an administrative assistant for a cardiologist at Massachusetts General Hospital in Boston, functions in a private setting on a one-to-one basis with the physician for whom she works. From her perspective as an employee in a hospital environment, she believes it is a very good, interesting, and rewarding field in which to be employed. The medical field is changing in the way medical services are delivered and in the type of insurance coverage there is for patients. Secretarial roles also differ depending on whether the work is in a hospital, in a private setting, or in a clinic in a hospital. Nicosia handles practically everything for her boss. Some of her responsibilities are the following:

- Make appointments for patients, including admissions for cardiac catheterization and surgery, and coordinate other appointments such as tests that include exercise or vascular studies and neurology
- Transcribe 75 percent of the recorded dictation for the physician (The load of documents is excessive and it must be completed expeditiously, so approximately 25 percent of it is sent to a transcription service.)
- Access patients' test results from the computer
- Prepare a preliminary report for the physician's review of tests taken—such as a stress test—a few hours after they have been performed
- Coordinate appointments with other physicians
- Pick up a medical record for signature and then return it to the appropriate station
- Maintain a copy of lectures presented by the physician and then update it as necessary
- Keep physician's CV current
- Coordinate the physician's meetings
- Arrange for weekend coverage if the physician is not available

To work in a medical environment, you need to be well organized, have good keyboarding and computer skills, be well versed in spelling, be flexible, have good telephone manners, have a pleasant approach, and be able to think and plan ahead. As you remain in this position, you keep learning and assume more and more responsibility.

If you are interested in a profession in the medical environment, Nicosia advises continuing your education and enrolling in a medical secretarial/administrative curriculum for at least a two-year degree and more, if possible. In this type of program, you will learn medical terminology, which would be very beneficial, and clinical procedures, too.

Technical

A technical secretary works for a scientist or an engineer, employers who are generally found in the laboratory rather than in the office. Therefore, the secretary is more of an administrative assistant who is in charge of organizing and implementing most of the office routines. In addition to the usual secretarial duties, the technical secretary prepares most of the correspondence from composing to mailing; maintains the technical library; and gathers, types, and edits materials for scientific papers. The engineering secretary checks specifications in contracts against standards and orders the materials that meet the specifications.

Opportunities are best for the technical secretary who has knowledge of the technology and vocabulary relevant to a specific field, familiarity with mathematical and/or engineering symbols, skills in formatting and keyboarding statistical tables, and high standards of performance in production of technical reports. A good knowledge of and interest in mathematics and science contribute to job satisfaction and success. Besides work in professional offices, jobs are available in industry. Some of the fields for which you can prepare as a technical secretary are in electronics, communications, aerospace, nuclear energy, and ecology.

Educational

Educational secretaries may work in a variety of institutions: private or public elementary, intermediate, or high schools; two- or four-year colleges; and universities. If you like working in an educational environment, then you also may have a choice of location. Do you prefer a small town, a large city, or a college town?

School secretaries may work directly with administrators and teachers. They meet and talk with parents, business leaders, visitors, community representatives, board members, and others who are involved with the school. Duties of the position may range from taking dictation and keyboarding correspondence and documents to taking minutes of meetings, preparing governmental reports, and ordering and distributing supplies.

Public schools in some cities require applicants for positions to pass an examination. Therefore, you should investigate this requirement in the area where you wish to find a job.

Private Secretarial Service

For secretaries who wish to operate their own businesses, secretarial services might be the answer. These firms perform a wide range of services for the public such as keyboarding correspondence, reports, proposals, manuals, repetitive letters, database input, and graphs on a computer; desktop publishing; composing, formatting, and typing résumés; taking telephone and tape transcription; handling mail (folding, stuffing, sealing, affixing postage); printing labels; notarizing documents; and handling faxes.

To run a business successfully, you need good marketing and management skills as well as the ability to determine charges for different types of projects, which includes determining overhead, expenses, cost of equipment, insurance, and supplies. In addition, you should be familiar with the needs of the area in which you plan to offer services. Such a business can be home-based, conducted in a storefront, or located in a professional building. This is an excellent small business venture for those who have previous professional secretarial experience because they have the right mix of technical, administrative, and interpersonal skills.

What are some of the advantages for the user of these services? The owner of a newly established business, for example, may employ a secretarial service because it is less expensive than hiring permanent clerical staff.

Public Stenographer

The public stenographer is another kind of service rendered by secretaries who wish to run their own businesses. The offices usually are located in a hotel near prospective employers who need special services in a hurry. Public stenographers serve only those who bring work to them; and because they usually do only small jobs for a traveling population of employers, they can charge rather high rates for piecework. Public stenographers are usually also notary publics, those authorized by the state to witness signatures. They receive a small fee for this service. Much of their work is of a legal nature, and secretaries contemplating careers as public stenographers should be experienced in legal work.

The major advantages of becoming a public stenographer are freedom from supervision and a wide variety of work assignments. One never knows what type of job will come in, and you can make a very good salary if you are located in a high-paying area. The disadvantages are the instability of employment and the possibility of low income during holiday periods and slack seasons, or of working in a poor location. Public stenography demands a high degree of skill and flexibility, for each new employer is different, with unique demands and requirements.

Court Reporter

The opportunities in court reporting are varied and plentiful. It is a highly challenging profession for a person who has knowledge of specialized terminology in the legal, medical, insurance, and engineering fields. The court reporter must also be a good communicator, computer literate, well organized, able to meet deadlines, and able to work well under pressure.

Court reporters typically create verbatim transcripts of speeches, conversations, legal proceedings, meetings, and other events when written accounts of spoken words are necessary for correspondence, records, or legal proof. They play a critical role not only in judicial proceedings, but also at every meeting where the spoken word must be preserved as a written transcript. They are responsible for ensuring a complete, accurate, and secure legal record. In addition to preparing and protecting the legal record, many court reporters assist judges and trial attorneys in a variety of ways, such as organizing and searching for information in the official record or making suggestions to judges and attorneys regarding courtroom administration and procedure. Increasingly, court reporters are providing closed-captioning and real-time translating services to the deaf and hard-of-hearing community.

There are several methods of court reporting. The most common method is called *stenographic*. Stenotypists document all statements made in official proceedings using a stenotype machine, which allows them to press multiple keys simultaneously to record combinations representing sounds, words, or phrases. The symbols are electronically recorded and then translated and displayed as text in a process called *computer-aided transcription.*

In real-time court reporting, stenotype machines used for real-time captioning are linked directly to a computer. As the reporter keys in the symbols, they instantly appear as text on the screen. This process, called *communications access realtime translation* (CART), is used in courts, in classrooms, at meetings, and for closed captioning for the hearing-impaired on television.

Electronic reporting refers to the use of audio equipment to record court proceedings. The court reporter monitors the process, takes notes to identify speakers, and listens to the recording to ensure clarity and quality. The equipment used may include analog tape recorders or digital equipment. Electronic reporters and transcribers often are responsible for producing a subsequent written transcript of the recorded proceeding.

Another method of court reporting is called *voice writing.* Using this method, a court reporter speaks directly into a voice silencer, which is a handheld mask containing a microphone. As the reporter repeats the testimony into the recorder, the mask prevents the reporter from being heard during testimony. Voice writers record everything that is said by judges, witnesses, attorneys, and other parties to a proceeding, including gestures and emotional reactions.

Regardless of the method used, accuracy in court reporting is crucial because the court reporter is the only person creating an official transcript. In a judicial setting, for example, appeals often depend on the court reporter's transcript.

The amount of training required to become a court reporter varies with the type of reporting chosen. It usually takes less than a year to become a voice writer, while electronic reporters and transcribers learn their skills on the job. In contrast, the average length of time it takes to become a stenotypist is thirty-three months. Training is offered by about 160 postsecondary vocational and technical schools and colleges. The National Court Reporters Association (NCRA) has approved approximately seventy programs, all of which offer courses in stenotype computer-aided transcription and real-time reporting. NCRA-approved programs require students to capture a minimum of 225 words per minute, a requirement for federal government employment as well.

6

Is Administrative Work for You?

ADMINISTRATIVE ASSISTANTS CONTINUE to make a difference in today's business world. Changes that affect the office environment are moving at speeds of lightning. To enjoy the career you select, you need to move with the times. You must develop your skills not only to include the mastery of computer software and the latest technology, but also to develop leadership, organizational, interpersonal, problem-solving, and communication competencies. You need to be flexible, able to adjust to constant change, and understand and enjoy a diverse workforce and the culture employees bring to the workplace. Take advantage of all opportunities to enhance your skills, to gain knowledge, and to make yourself a valuable member of the firm. Keep in mind that administrative assistants are now assuming many of the responsibilities that were previously performed by managers.

When making decisions about a career, you undoubtedly should select one that is satisfying, enjoyable, and at which you can perform well. Some of the factors you should evaluate in selecting a career are your likes and dislikes for certain kinds of work, the opportunities within the field, promotional paths for upward mobility, earning power, socialization, and employment opportunities that exist now as well as in the future.

Probably the single most important advantage in planning an administrative career is knowing that a great need exists for this category of office work. Even during periods of recession, the demand for administrative assistants is high because of the tremendous amounts of paperwork that companies must process. Another advantage of this type of work is the diversity of options that are available in selecting executive and administrative work or specialties, such as legal, educational, or medical. Or, you may decide to become self-employed and be a successful entrepreneur, open your own secretarial services business, or become a freelance transcriptionist.

In addition, alternative schedules to the traditional nine-to-five workday are now operative in firms across the country. If you are a busy homemaker, you may choose to work part-time, or if you enjoy learning about many companies, you can work as a temporary employee. Still more interesting is flextime for those who want to work around family responsibilities. Another advantage is to choose an alternative location for your workplace, a direction in which many firms are now going, rather than the office setting where you normally carried out the responsibilities of the job. See Chapter 4 for more information.

On the other hand, while technological progress has led to many advances in administrative work, it has also made it easier for employees to work longer hours. According to the Steelcase Survey, an annual survey that measures workplace trends in the United States, in 2005, 55 percent of office workers took a lunch break of thirty minutes or fewer. The survey also suggests women are much more likely to take shorter lunches than men (61 percent versus 48 percent). The survey indicates that a changed work environment, increased pressure to perform, and the desire to leave earlier at the end of the day are contributing factors to this change. Additionally, 21 percent of respondents use the time for individual work because more time is now spent working in teams.[1]

The results of the Steelcase survey reveal that only 61 percent of Americans use all of their allotted vacation time and almost half of the respondents (43 percent) spent at least some time working during their vacations. This is a trend that is growing significantly; those who report working while on vacation have nearly doubled (from 23 percent) in the ten years since the last survey.

When asked the reasons why they work while on vacation, the majority of respondents reported it is because they are "committed to the job" (25 percent) or have "a pressing assignment that needs to be taken care of" (22 percent). Additional reasons for working on vacation include "don't want to leave it all for when I get back" (12 percent), "technology makes it easy" (11 percent), and the inability to "relax until things are taken care of" (10 percent).[2]

---

1. Beautyman, Mairi. "Steelcase Survey: Lunch Hour Lost. Women Take Shorter Lunches Than Men." *Interior Design,* July 28, 2005. http://www.interiordesign.net/id_news article/ca630335.html, June 28, 2006.

2. "Steelcase Workplace Index Survey Reveals Growing Trend of Working on Vacation." http://www.prnewswire.com/cgi-bin/stories.pl?acct=109&story=/www/story/07-20-2006/0004400513&edate=, July 28, 2006.

Trends in Office Environments

Dramatic advances in office automation have provided a new world of opportunities for administrative careers. No longer are jobs necessarily dead-end clerical positions. New avenues of career progression have opened up for those who keep updated in skills and knowledge. Administrative workstations contain the hardware and software for multifunctional responsibilities such as word processing, data processing, telecommunications, presentation graphics, and spreadsheets. Workstations are integrated through local area networks, and administrative assistants have access to the Internet and communicate through e-mail. Administrative job responsibilities are growing and expanding in direct relation to the sophistication of the equipment these personnel operate.

The rate of growth is good and is opening up more diversified career opportunities that require different attitudes and skills, higher-level decision making and problem-solving abilities, and new knowledge qualifications. A question pertaining to these new designs is: Who will manage these systems? Undoubtedly, the person who qualifies for such positions will have to understand the broad concepts of office systems, management, productivity, and personnel administration.

Another trend in office environments that has implications for finding more meaningful work experiences is the growth of departments of human resources. Management has shifted its emphasis from the sole use of technology to increase productivity to the more efficient use of people. This leads to good human relationships among staff hierarchy, which ultimately results in greater job satisfaction, a feeling of belonging, and the use of more creative and interpersonal skills.

Departments of human resources focus on management of people rather than administration of policies and procedures, and they make an organized effort to match people with jobs. They assess the skills, knowledge, and abilities of personnel and encourage personal growth. Many firms also incorporate career counseling and training in their programs.

Insuring personnel—an important company function—has led to the need to improve work environments. Work space, equipment, and furniture are ergonomically designed to accommodate the needs of people as well as the task, resulting in more attractive surroundings that serve the psychological and physiological requirements of the workers.

Another factor that has had an impact on the office is the fact that information is now considered as much a corporate resource as are the plant and equipment. Information and communication are almost synonymous terms as technology continues to make more interconnection possible. Office administration is now considered as important to a company as are, say, marketing and finance.

Advancement Opportunities

The number of traditional secretaries began to decrease from the time word processing was first introduced, and secretaries who primarily worked in automated offices began to support more than one principal. With downsizing, they also began to assume many responsibilities formerly performed by managers. Advancement came with these responsibilities. According to the International Association of Administrative Professionals (IAAP), "Companies are creating a multitude of career paths for persons in office/administrative professions. Secretaries have moved into training, supervision, desktop publishing, information management, and research."

Secretaries should have a technical and conceptional knowledge of the field and an understanding of the business operations of an organization. Interestingly, secretaries were the ones initially trained to become managers of word processing centers.

In addition to supervisory and managerial opportunities, you also have a lateral career option, which is to switch from jobs with one type of responsibility to another, such as from computer operator to trainer.

For more information on the advancement opportunities available to you as an administrative assistant, see Chapter 9.

Teamwork Is In!

Today, self-managed work teams are replacing the formerly autocratic, from-the-top-down management style. This type of team management enables employees at all levels in an organization to participate and share responsibility for implementing organizational goals. Group work settings support a more participative culture, an enhanced exchange of information, and greater levels of team interaction. Surveys indicate that increased productivity is an offshoot of teamwork. If you are part of an office professional team, you, as well as the other members of your team, must understand what is expected of you—your roles and responsibilities—and how you can make a contribution to the department or firm. Teams are usually involved in the administrative functions of planning, organizing, and complex problem solving; and each member of the team develops the collaborative skills needed to work with the group. Employees gain empowerment as they work in these teams, and they learn to manage themselves.

What are the skills and personal qualities that administrative assistants need to demonstrate as part of a successful team? First and most important is a commitment to company goals. Other skills and qualities are the following:

- Communicating frequently with all members of the team and appropriate managers
- Listening effectively, considering contributions of others, and separating fact from emotion
- Identifying and solving problems
- Keeping up to date
- Suggesting ideas and procedures for implementing them

An administrative assistant and a manager can also constitute a team. An assistant who takes the initiative can make things happen by recognizing opportunities to improve, change, create, and contribute to the work environment. You can use these various means to familiarize yourself with all aspects of the organization, volunteer for jobs other than what is expected of you in your position, keep learning to add to your storehouse of knowledge, and contribute to a productive and harmonious working environment. Effective teamwork leads to improvement in a company's productive operations and to more satisfied employees who have gained a professional identity within the organization.

Older Workers in the Job Market

Many personnel experts believe that workers beyond the age of fifty have a competitive edge in the job market. They usually have had previous experience with several employers and are looked up to as role models by younger workers. The older employee conveys an image of stability. Until recently, mature individuals had been returning to the job market for several reasons: an inflationary economy bringing about a need for additional family income; self-fulfillment; boredom after children grow up; changing social values; and the women's liberation movement.

Mature individuals have many opportunities to find employment. A number of these workers come from professional backgrounds that have provided them with a wealth of experience and knowledge that they can bring to a new position. Older workers often opt for part-time employment, either to supplement a pension or as a way to keep a hand in the workforce after early retirement. A number of older workers choose to enter administrative careers as full-time employees after retiring early from a previous occupation.

Other such workers are returning to the workforce after a long period of unemployment. This is often the case for women who decide to return to work after raising a family. Many in this position choose part-time employment as a way to ease back into the work environment and update their skills.

With the need for qualified administrative staff in so many industries, the returning adult who has a sense of responsibility and loyalty and who possesses good skills should have no difficulty finding and keeping a job. These adults should enlist in continuing education courses to update their skills, abilities, and knowledge.

U.S. Department of Labor statistics indicate that older workers will be the fastest-growing segment of the labor force. By 2010, 17 percent of the workforce is expected to be age fifty-five and older. Two-thirds of workers from ages forty-five to seventy-four report that they plan to continue to work after retirement. Another 6.6 million workers are added from those aged fifty-five to sixty-four.

In Canada, the proportion of women in federal public service aged forty-five or older rose in 2004 to 39 percent from 35 percent in 1998. However, the proportion was lower than that for men aged forty-five or older, which rose to 49 percent from 46 percent.

Many adult training centers, public schools, private business institutions, and colleges have developed one-year certificate programs for the adult who wants to return to school. These adults may enroll in refresher courses or may learn specialized skills in office technology. Some schools even have cooperative work programs where students work in industry for a stipulated period of time each week. This experience enables the mature adult who has been a homemaker for many years to become accustomed to the working environment and to get a broad view of the changes that have occurred.

Advantages of Working as an Administrative Assistant

In previous years, secretarial work was often perceived in a negative light. "She is 'only' a secretary" was an image that kept many qualified individuals from entering the field. However, through the hard work of professional secretarial organizations and changes brought about in business with the advent of technological environments, which created secretarial specialists as well as supervisory and managerial positions for secretaries, this image began to fade.

As secretaries have evolved into administrative professionals, their image has fortunately begun to change. Administrative assistants and other office professionals are now highly regarded for their skills and contribution to the company.

The International Association of Administrative Professionals has compiled a list of reasons why you should be glad that you've chosen to pursue this interesting profession. Here is a description of their reasons.[3]

- Your skill set is broader than that of most managers and other professionals, which means that you can more easily move into a different department or new industry.
- Technology is the basis for most administrative tasks, making support personnel primary technology users, who are often asked to teach new software techniques and troubleshoot any computer problems.
- As technological advances continue to evolve, those with the best skills will find the best advancement opportunities and highest salaries.
- The need to keep up with technology is an excellent reason to pursue continuing education and training. Administrative professionals can justify company-sponsored learning expenses more readily than can other workers.
- It is easier for companies to upgrade an administrative position by increasing salary to keep up with increasing responsibilities than to downgrade managerial positions by reducing pay, status, and duties.
- Your willingness to adapt, grow, and keep learning is even more important than your current skills. A positive attitude will take you a long way in the workplace.

---

3. IAAP, "Reasons to Be Glad You're an Administrative Professional." http://www.iaap hq.org/researchtrends/reasons_to_be_an_ admin_professional.htm, July 2, 2006.

- You are comfortable using the valuable skills of diplomacy, tact, influence, and negotiation to get a job done.
- Even if your technology skills are rusty, your people skills have become more important as new forms of communication become available.
- As executives are faced with increasing workloads, they are realizing the powerful effectiveness of a skilled administrator in running an office.

Salaries

In Chapter 4 you read about starting salary statistics for different administrative professional careers and median earnings by region. The Bureau of Labor Statistics reports that in May 2004, median annual earnings of executive secretaries and administrative assistants were $34,970. The majority earned between $28,500 and $43,430, while the lowest 10 percent earned less than $23,810, and the highest 10 percent earned more than $53,460.

Median annual earnings of legal secretaries were $36,720 in May 2004, with most earning between $29,070 and $46,390. The lowest 10 percent earned less than $23,270, and the highest 10 percent earned more than $56,590.

Medical secretaries earned a median annual salary of $26,540. The middle 50 percent earned between $21,980 and $32,690, while the lowest 10 percent earned less than $19,140, and the highest 10 percent earned more than $39,140.

For all other secretaries, median annual earnings were $26,110 in May 2004.

Median annual earnings in the industries employing the largest numbers of executive secretaries and administrative assistants in May 2004 were:

Management of companies and enterprises—$38,950
Local government—$36,940
Colleges, universities, and professional schools—$34,280
Employment services—$31,620
State government—$30,750

Secretarial salaries have been rising each year. All indications are that there is a bright, exciting future for this career field.

A Broadening Field

There has been a movement for women to leave traditionally female occupations for those that were once exclusively filled by men. As for males entering the administrative profession, they are beginning to see the opportunities and satisfaction that they can derive, particularly with the invasion of technology and systems in office environments. The future may be more promising, and we may see more men entering the profession for the following reasons: as firms delete the word *secretary* from titles, men will not feel the "stigma" attached to the job and become candidates for available positions; jobs are available now and projected to continue in the future; automation is creating many opportunities for advancement; challenges for systems and innovation and creativity exist; and supervisory and managerial positions with varied titles and responsibilities appeal to the upwardly mobile.

Finley A. Lanier Jr., who began his career as a secretary in a word processing department and has been in the profession for a long time, states:

> The profession was intriguing since very few males sought entrance, and I wanted to secure a future with skills that would

be helpful in landing a job. I have found it to be rather challenging and stressful at times. Serving others and being on top of things and networking with counterparts are only a few of the rewards achieved from this career. When one can take pride in the accomplishments in a day's work and know that as a result you have added a dimension to the situation, this really is gratifying.

Some advice Lanier gives to be successful is that "A secretary must stay out of office politics, avoid arguments, and remember that you are there to serve a purpose and to get the job done. That is the only thing that matters."

Another interesting factor that might reverse this notion of "female occupation" is the trend toward workstations where executives are now being forced to perform keyboarding functions once exclusively within the secretary's domain. Reluctantly, executives are learning to "key-in" their own requests on their own terminals. This, too, should bring about a different set of attitudes about secretarial work.

Key Roles

Increasing office automation and organizational restructuring will continue to make secretaries and administrative assistants more productive in coming years, as computers, e-mail, scanners, and voice message systems allow them to accomplish more in the same amount of time.

Developments in office technology are certain to continue, and they will bring about further changes in the work of secretaries and administrative assistants. However, many secretarial and administrative duties are of a personal, interactive nature and, therefore, they cannot be easily automated. Responsibilities such as planning conferences, working with clients, instructing staff, and dealing with subordinates require excellent tact and communication skills. Because technology cannot substitute for these personal skills, secretaries and administrative assistants will continue to play a key role in most organizations.

7

EDUCATIONAL PREPARATION FOR ADMINISTRATIVE ASSISTANTS

YOU MAY QUALIFY for entry-level secretarial positions as a high school graduate with basic office skills. However, bear in mind that employers increasingly require extensive knowledge of software applications, such as word processing, spreadsheets, and database management.

To succeed as a secretary or administrative assistant, you should be proficient in keyboarding and good at spelling, punctuation, grammar, and oral communication. Employers also look for good customer service and interpersonal skills. Discretion, good judgment, organizational or management ability, initiative, and the ability to work independently are especially important for higher-level administrative positions.

Educational and Other Requirements

As office automation continues to evolve, retraining and continuing education will remain integral parts of administrative jobs. Changes in the office environment have increased the demand for secretaries and administrative assistants who are both adaptable and versatile.

Although you just read that the minimum requirement for a secretarial position is graduation from high school, you also know that the advanced skills that most employers look for will require some additional education. You need to prepare yourself to compete with the population looking for employment. In a 2005 International Association of Administrative Professionals (IAAP) survey, 89 percent of respondents reported that they have at least some postsecondary education and/or have earned postsecondary academic degrees.

Postsecondary Education Achieved

College/university—some credit classes	24%
College/university—bachelor's degree	15%
Junior/community college—associate degree	16%
Junior/community college—some credit classes	13%
Business/technical school/college—2-year program	6%
Business/technical school/college—1-year program	3%
College/university—some postgraduate	3%
College/university—master's degree	2%
College/university—doctorate	1%
None	11%

In jobs where a degree is not required, college graduates who either do not find employment in their field or who choose to make a career switch will be a source of employment for these jobs. Therefore, you'll face greater competition for these jobs because employers may look upon these college graduates more favorably, particularly as skills needed in administrative positions become more complex. Some employers actually inflate the educational requirement for certain jobs because of the abundance of college graduates looking for work and because they anticipate grooming graduates for administrative and managerial positions.

Specific hiring requirements vary from firm to firm; however, many companies require a keying speed of sixty-five words per minute (wpm) and above seventy wpm for individuals in word processing areas. Knowledge of shorthand may be an asset in securing a well-paying job, particularly during periods when competition is keen and in large firms where higher-level executives and senior partners request it. In addition to general secretarial and specialized skills and knowledge, good organizational ability and knowledge of software applications, such as word processing, spreadsheet, database management, scanners, and information storage systems, will give you the leading edge in a competitive job market.

A continuous need has existed for specialized administrative assistants in legal, medical, and technical organizations. In these specialties you need a firm grounding in terminology, an understanding of the field, and knowledge of office procedures used in the specific kind of environment.

The continuing changes occurring in office environments because of technology affect equipment and procedures as well as skill and knowledge requirements. Concomitantly, new career paths and positions continue to be created that call for different combinations of skills, attitudes, and knowledge. Alert individuals who consider education as an ongoing process and as an integral part of the job will become prime candidates for these openings.

Is Shorthand Obsolete?

Opinions vary about the need for shorthand. Some believe it is necessary for secretarial employment; but since it is no longer used extensively, others believe it is becoming an archaic skill. Shorthand dictation is still used in some offices, particularly by executives who became accustomed to working routinely with a specific individual. Administrative and other office personnel use shorthand on a pretty steady basis for writing telephone messages, recording instructions, and taking minutes of meetings. Having a good shorthand skill is really a plus. When checking the help wanted ads in the *New York Times* under the categories of "administrative assistant," "executive assistant," and "secretary," none of the ads specified shorthand. However, a good number of higher-level executives and senior partners in law firms require shorthand. Individuals who are proponents of shorthand state that those individuals with shorthand skills average approximately an 18 percent higher salary than those without it. Job seekers with shorthand skills have a competitive edge over those lacking this skill in being hired in the better salaried jobs.

The above statements attest to the fact that the demand for shorthand has decreased considerably for general secretarial work; however, it is not yet obsolete. It is still a requirement in some higher-level administrative executive secretarial positions and in legal positions with partners. Shorthand skill is a plus and will open doors to positions in the executive suite.

Secretarial/Administrative Assistant Programs of Study

Secretarial education continues to be offered; however, the curriculum or program designation varies in each school. Courses of study are offered in high school vocational training centers and one- and two-year programs in business schools, vocational-technical institutions, and community colleges. In degree-granting institutions, students need to complete liberal arts as well as specialized courses. Review the curricula from the different schools and districts that are included in the text that follows. All of the examples included are from the state of New York; check your local schools for specific offerings in your area.

High School Programs

In the past, schools in a particular district would offer similar programs for the secretarial major. However, there is no consistency now in New York State, and requirements for liberal arts and business courses vary from school to school because of the added state requirements in the academic areas. This has affected the number of electives that can be selected from the field of business. Each school district is now tailoring these electives to meet its local needs.

In schools equipped with personal computers, students generally learn to keyboard on this equipment. In Nanuet High School in Nanuet, New York, which has the latest technology, students learn the computer keyboard in the first semester. Students who are majoring in the secretarial field take a second semester of keyboarding, where in addition to developing their keyboarding skills, they do production work that includes correspondence and reports.

Some basic English is also taught. In the third semester, business computer applications are presented and students learn word processing, set up a database, and learn a spreadsheet. Included in the instructions are rough drafts, endnotes, superscripts, and other types of notations. Advanced computer work is presented in the fourth semester, in which software packages such as Word, Powerpoint, Excel, Desktop Publishing, and Print Shop are introduced.

The business-education department in Ramapo Senior High School, Spring Valley, New York, which serves a large population, offers what it calls a Three-Unit Sequence and Model Five-Unit Sequences. Overall, the department offers thirty courses from which students have certain choices, based on the sequence they decide to follow. Some of them are computer courses, including keyboarding, word processing, spreadsheets, and desktop publishing; finance and law courses; marketing-management courses; mathematics courses; speedwriting; a retail-store academy; a work experience program; and its Career Exploration Internship Program (CEIP). Here are two examples of Ramapo's business-marketing education sequences.

Three-Unit Sequence Options
As the World Changes I & II (Introduction to
  Occupations) *or* As the World Changes I and one of the
  following:
  > Computers in Business
  > Keyboarding
Personal Keyboarding and Business Communications plus
  one of the following full-year courses:
  > Accounting
  > Business Communications and Personal Keyboarding

Business Law
College Accounting
College Business Law
Computers in Business
Computer Spreadsheets I & II
Keyboarding
Principles of Marketing
Record Keeping (Financial Information Processing)
Word Processing I & II (Electronic Information
   Processing)

Model Five-Unit Sequences

As the World Changes I & II (Introduction to
   Occupations)
Computers in Business
Personal Keyboarding and Business Communications plus
   any two courses listed below:

Marketing Cluster—
   Principles of Marketing
   Cooperative Work Experience

Financial Cluster—
   Accounting
   College Accounting
   Business Law
   Cooperative Work Experience

Information Cluster—
   Computers in Business
   Computer Spreadsheets I & II
   Word Processing I & II
   Cooperative Work Experience

Alternatives to the traditional forty-minute class period have been implemented in various high schools. Some now have block programs of two or three periods so that business situations can be simulated. Under this reorganization, students can complete tasks originated within the timeframe, rather than having to stop a project that is only partially completed. Some innovations also include simulated experiences in advanced keyboarding and office procedures classes. The advantage to this arrangement is that students see the interrelationships between different office jobs being performed. One of the benefits students derive in these simulated experiences is training in human relations, an aspect frequently neglected in more traditional classrooms.

Community College Programs

You should determine your long-range goals when you choose your career so that you are aware of the levels of education you need for positions with increasing responsibilities. With greater numbers of adults going on to college to earn degrees, you should think seriously about attending at least a two-year institution for post–high school education. Employers are beginning to seek college graduates to fill jobs. Since the early 1960s, two-year community colleges have expanded educational opportunities to provide the professions, business, and industry with qualified personnel.

Practically all these institutions offer secretarial programs, even if designated by another name, for which an associate in applied science (A.A.S.) degree can be earned. One such program for students that prepares them for secretarial/administrative assistant positions is given in the Secretarial Studies Program (sixty semester hours) of the Business and Information Systems Department at

Bronx Community College of The City University of New York. It is shown here in detail so you can see that students who successfully complete the program have the qualifications that will enable them to handle jobs with increasing responsibilities that were formerly done by managers.

Core Requirements
Fundamentals of Interpersonal Communication
Fundamentals of Written Composition I
History of the Modern World
Introduction to Mathematical Thought
Physical Education
Science

Required Areas of Study
Art Survey *or* Music Survey
Psychology *or* Sociology *or* Public Speaking and Critical
    Listening

Specialization Requirements
Business Communication
Business Mathematics *or* Introduction to Internet and Web
    Development
Information Processing Applications and Administration
Information Processing Office Simulation
Introduction to Business *or* Fundamental Accounting
Introduction to Desktop Publishing
Introduction to Office Automation Concepts *or*
    Multimedia Concepts and Applications for Business
Keyboarding I

Keyboarding II
Keyboarding III
Machine Transcription I
Machine Transcription II
Office Procedures
Senior Orientation
Supervision and Administration of Office Automation

Westchester Community College in Valhalla, New York, is part of the State University of New York education system. The school offers an A.A.S. degree (sixty-four semester hours) in office technologies that prepares students for office systems administration. Career areas include administrative assistant, office manager, sales assistant, customer service representative, and executive assistant.

Core Requirements
Behavioral Science, Humanities, *or* Social Science
Composition and Literature I and II
English 101, 102
Liberal Arts elective
Mathematics
Physical Education
Science

Degree Requirements
Business Communications
Business electives
Business Organization and Management
Computer Information Systems
Financial Accounting *or* Computerized Accounting I

Integrated Office Applications
Keyboarding and Information Processing
Office Administration
Spreadsheet and Database Applications *or* Management
   Information Systems
Word Processing Applications, both basic and advanced
   courses

A rather unique associate of arts degree in business, a two-year program, was developed at Indiana University of Pennsylvania, which is part of Pennsylvania's State System of Higher Education. The objectives in designing such a program were to provide business occupational education with the opportunity for specialization in computer and office information systems, to enable students to accept positions in this field, to upgrade knowledge and skills, and to provide the foundation for continuing in a four-year degree program. The A.A. program consists of the following courses:

Major Business (Associate) Core Required Courses
Accounting Principles I
Accounting Principles II
Business Technical Writing
Electronic Office Procedures
Essentials of Finance
Foundations of Business Mathematics
Introduction to Business
Introduction to Business Law
Introduction to Management Information Systems
Introduction to Microcomputers
Keyboarding and Document Formatting

Other Requirements (Computer and Office Specialization)
Business Applications
Business Computer Application Project
Business Systems Analysis and Design
Word Processing Applications

Specialized Secretarial Areas

An A.A.S. degree can be earned in the specialized secretarial fields, too; however, you must research the college catalogs to find out which two-year institutions have programs for legal, medical, educational, or technical secretaries. You may also check the catalogs of colleges that offer both an associate in science degree (A.S.) as well as a four-year bachelor of science degree (B.S.).

Legal Specialty

A specialized A.A.S. program for legal careers is offered in the Office Technology–Legal Department at Nassau Community College in Garden City, New York. Skills and knowledge related to a law office that students learn are speedwriting, machine transcription of legal documents, administrative management principles, and legal-office procedures. The legal curriculum is listed below.

First Semester
Activity course(s)
Administrative Management
College Keyboarding I
Composition I
Speedwriting I
Word Processing Applications I

Second Semester
Activity course(s)
Business Writing
Elective
Legal-Office Procedures I
Speedwriting II
Word Processing Applications II

Third Semester
Health elective
Legal-Office Procedures II
Legal Workshop
Mathematics elective
Shorthand Transcription I or Machine Transcription I
Social Science elective

Fourth Semester
Humanities elective
Lab Science elective
Legal Work/Study
Office Technology elective
Social Science elective

Medical Specialty

A medical curriculum in the Secretarial/Office Information Systems Program (sixty credits required for an A.A.S. degree) of the business department is offered at Bronx Community College of The City University of New York. These students may work in a variety of physicians' offices, hospitals, clinics, and laboratories. Students learn to transcribe medical documents from recorded dictation, complete medical forms, maintain office records, and manage a medical office. They learn how to use several software programs and become familiar with medical terminology and clinical techniques. Emphasis is also placed on secretarial, communications, and human relations skills, as recommended by the American Association of Medical Assistants. The curriculum is as follows.

First Semester
Business Mathematics
Fundamentals of Written Composition I
History of the Modern World
Human Biology
Keyboarding I

Second Semester
Information Processing Application and Administration
Introduction to Business
Introduction to Mathematical Thought
Keyboarding II
Machine Transcription I
Medical Terminology

Third Semester
Clinical Techniques I
Critical Issues in Health
Fundamentals of Interpersonal Communication
Introduction to Art *or* Introduction to Music
Keyboarding III
Psychology

Fourth Semester
Business Communications
Clinical Techniques II
Information Processing Office Simulation
Medical Law
Medical-Office Procedures and Management
Physical Education (activity course)
Senior Orientation

Web Design

With the proliferation of e-business today, more and more administrative professionals are becoming skilled in Web design and applications. The Department of Computer Information Systems and Office Technology at Westchester Community College in New York offers a certificate program in Web development for e-commerce that consists of thirty to thirty-three semester hours. The programming courses can be applied to the A.A.S. degree in computer information systems, and several computer graphics courses can be applied to either the A.A.S. degree in visual arts or the certificate in computer arts. Graduates of this certificate program will be qualified to seek employment as Web programmers, Web applications administrators, website coordinators, and webmasters in related occupations.

First Semester
Computer Graphics *or* Computer Photo Image
Marketing Elective
Object-Oriented Programming Logic

Second Semester
Database Management Systems
Internet Technologies *or* Telecommunications for
    Business
Introduction to Web Page Design

Third Semester
Advanced Web Design
C++ Programming for Business *or* Java Program for
    Business
Website Design and Management
Web Systems Analysis and Design

Private Colleges and Business Schools

In addition to the public community colleges, private two-year colleges as well as private business schools offer one- and two-year secretarial programs. You may wish to check on the accreditation of these schools before enrolling. Private business schools are also a primary source for business training. In many of them, students may enroll at any time, not necessarily at the beginning of the term, and may progress at their own rate.

Continuing Education Programs

In addition to the schools already mentioned, secretarial courses are offered in almost all continuing education programs in colleges, in evening high schools, at YMCAs, and wherever self-development is a major objective.

Internships

Other learning experiences are through internship programs or cooperative work experience. This experience helps bridge the gap between college and the real world. Generally, classroom study is combined with supervised on-the-job work. Students may be placed in internships for one semester, but they also attend weekly seminars at the college and share job experiences and features of the work environment. In cooperative work experience programs, arrangements vary. Sometimes students work part-time while attending college, or they may work for a certain block of time and then return to the college. The coordinator usually identifies job openings, arranges interviews, and supervises students. Well-run programs match student skills and interests to employer needs.

Company-Sponsored Programs

Company-sponsored programs are also conducted to provide opportunities for additional learning or reinforcement of skills that are relevant to company activities. Frequently, when a considerable number of employees are deficient in certain kinds of knowledge or skills, as perceived by supervisors or by employees themselves, courses are designed to meet these needs.

Once you are established in a job and sense new needs that are shared by others in your department or skill area, it is sometimes possible to initiate training programs in your company. If you have a good idea that would benefit the company as well as the workers, write a brief proposal and talk it over with your immediate superior. Give that person a chance to discuss it with the personnel department or with her or his supervisor. It is much more likely to receive a favorable response if you follow channels and are polite and businesslike about making the proposal. Some examples of times that such a proposal might be appropriate are when the company would benefit from using new types of equipment such as computers or printers. It bears repeating that the important factor is whether the company will benefit by the proposed training program. More information on company training programs is given in Chapter 9.

Secretarial Programs in Canada

The nature and level of skills required in the labor market have changed in Canada as in the United States. Computer technology is needed for word processing, spreadsheets, database management, desktop publishing, and information storage. Administrative assistants need to have excellent keyboarding, communications, English, organizational, and analytical skills. The technological innovations have changed the way work is done, who does it, and the skills required. To prepare youth for employment, the government's long-term goal is "to make cooperative education programs available in every high school in Canada."

In Canada, secretarial jobs are the largest group of information-based jobs in the economy. If employed in a specialized area such as medicine, law, or commerce, it is necessary to understand the technical language. Similar to the United States, the basic requirement for entry-level secretarial positions is high school graduation. Some employers are looking for individuals who have earned a secretarial career certificate or have completed a college-level office program. The demand is growing for individuals with a college education. Those graduates from related fields of business, commerce, management, and administration, including university graduates, compete for secretarial jobs when they cannot find employment in their field of study.

Some of the programs offered at the Open Learning Agency and at most colleges are secretarial, word processing, computer application, legal, and medical secretarial preparation. For those interested in supervisory and administrative positions, administrative programs are available. The prerequisites for admission into the secretarial career field in community colleges vary from institution to institution. Generally, candidates must pass an English proficiency test and must have completed advanced English courses at the high school level, must meet established typing and shorthand standards, and they frequently are required to pass an interview. The two-year program is offered in all community colleges in all of the provinces, with the exception of one or two depending on the course of study.

Secretaries, recorders, and transcriptionists work in government and throughout the private sector including law offices, company legal departments, real estate companies, land titles offices, courts, doctors' offices, hospitals, clinics, and other medical organizations. This occupational group also includes executive, private, and technical secretaries; estate, medical, legal, litigation, and real estate secretaries; court reporters; and stenographers.

The speed at which technology is moving and the impact it has on the office environment and office occupations stress the importance of lifetime learning.

8

Professional Organizations and Certification

Like any other field, the administrative profession makes available to its members a variety of resources as well as the means by which recognition and advancement can be achieved.

Professional Administrative Organizations

There are several organizations that administrative professionals can join to interact with colleagues, enhance their skills, attend workshops and seminars, and keep current on what's happening in the profession.

International Association of Administrative Professionals (IAAP)

The International Association of Administrative Professionals is the world's leading organization for secretaries and administrative staff and has six hundred chapters and approximately forty thousand members in more than sixty-six countries. This organization sponsors seminars and workshops at the local, state, and national levels that are organized to develop the personal and professional expertise of administrative assistants. The organization sponsors a Future Secretaries Association Program, mostly at the high school level, to inform students about the secretarial profession and to interest them in entering the field. One of the primary educational activities of the IAAP is the administration of the Certified Professional Secretaries (CPS) program. The Research and Educational Foundation provides funds for projects that benefit secretaries, management, and the educational field. In addition, the organization publishes nine issues per year of *The Secretary,* which is mailed to all members.

National Association of Legal Secretaries (NALS)

The National Association of Legal Secretaries is the association for legal professionals. It offers professional development by providing continuing legal education, certifications, information, and training to those choosing to make their careers in the legal services industry. NALS members represent every area of this industry from paralegals and legal assistants to legal administrators and office managers.

Legal secretaries are eligible for membership in the National Association of Legal Secretaries (International), which has more than six thousand members nationwide. Its mission statement reads that it "is dedicated to enhancing the competencies and contributions of members in the legal services profession." It accomplishes its mission and supports the public interest through the following:

- Continuing legal education and resource materials
- Networking opportunities at the local, state, regional, and national levels
- Commitment to a code of ethics and professional standards
- Professional certification programs and designations

The organization also sponsors a professional examination and certifying program. You may be asking yourself how you will benefit from being a NALS member. Most important is to make friends and contacts in the profession with whom you may share ideas and experiences. You also receive a copy of the *NALS Law* magazine four times a year. As a member, you may attend seminars and educational programs held locally and throughout the United States. The Continuing Legal Education Council plans programs on the national level.

American Association of Medical Assistants (AAMA)

Medical assistants in the United States and Canada should become members of the American Association of Medical Assistants. It is an association of individuals including medical secretaries, receptionists, medical office managers, and other medical professionals who work in health-care environments. The organization is dedicated to the professional advancement of its constituents.

The AAMA has more than four hundred chapters with a membership over twenty thousand. As a member, you are entitled to participate in its continuing education services, usually seminars and workshops, for which you can earn continuing education unit (CEU) credit. Another way to earn CEU credit is by successfully completing examinations that accompany the guided study programs. These are home-study courses that enable medical assistants to work independently at their own rate of speed. Three courses are now available: Law for the Medical Office, Human Relations, and Urinalysis Today.

An official bimonthly journal, *The Professional Medical Assistant*, and the *AAMA Network*, a quarterly newsletter, are other benefits of membership.

Because of the nature of the profession, the organization recognizes that members face ethical dilemmas daily; therefore, they developed the AAMA Code of Ethics, which is part of the organization's bylaws. The responsibilities enumerated within are service for the dignity of humanity, respect for confidentiality, maintenance of the high honor and principles of the profession, continued study to improve knowledge and skills of medical assistants, and participation in services to improve the community. Complete information about the AAMA is available at www.aama-ntl.org.

American Association for Medical Transcription (AAMT)

Another professional medical organization to join is the American Association for Medical Transcription. Transcriptionists are usually employed in medical institutions. The AAMT provides opportunities for networking, training, and continuing education for its members in the United States and Canada. Visit its website at www.aamt.org for information.

Ontario Medical Secretaries Association (OMSA)

In Ontario, Canada, medical secretaries are eligible for membership in the Ontario Medical Secretaries Association. This is a provincial organization whose primary goal is to expand the knowledge base of its members and keep them abreast of rapidly changing office methods and equipment. The association sponsors a certification program for qualified applicants to achieve professional status as a Certified Medical Secretary (CMS).

National Association of Educational Office Professionals

Educational secretaries may belong to the National Association of Educational Office Professionals. This group works for increased recognition for educational office personnel. It sponsors a professional standards program (PSP) to encourage members to grow professionally and to keep up to date in the profession and field of education. It also has an awards program in which it honors outstanding administrators and office professionals, individuals for distinguished service, and affiliated associations for outstanding newsletters and magazines. A benefit along with membership is *The National Educational Secretary*, which is published four times a year.

Association of Business Support Services International (ABSSI)

The Association of Business Support Services International represents secretarial service owners and managers. It has twelve hundred members and forty state groups. Active membership is granted to businesses that are engaged in full-time services. The association publishes a newsletter that includes diverse articles pertaining to the membership's type of business. It also holds workshops and seminars and shares referrals and training. For information about this organization, visit www.abssi.org.

Association of Information Systems Professionals (AISP)

The Association of Information Systems Professionals is an information management organization with local chapters throughout the United States. It sponsors an annual symposium and publishes valuable literature.

Association of Records Managers and Administrators (ARMA)

The Association of Records Managers and Administrators has approximately eleven thousand members, including records managers, archivists, corporate librarians, imaging specialists, legal professionals, IT managers, consultants, and educators, all of whom work in a wide variety of industries, including government, legal, health care, financial services, and petroleum in the United States, Canada, and thirty-plus other countries.

Certification and Licensing

The two organizations that sponsor examinations to certify secretaries are the International Association of Administrative Professionals and the National Association of Legal Secretaries. The IAAP offers certification to secretaries in the United States and Canada; NALS serves those in the United States only. A secretary who earns certification is usually a highly motivated person who has superior skills and knowledge. This is viewed by other professionals and employers as a level of achievement that warrants recognition. For secretaries, certification is equal in importance to the CPA designation for accountants. Therefore, if you want to reach the highest level in the secretarial profession, you should work toward this achievement.

Certified Professional Secretary (CPS) and Certified Administrative Professional (CAP)

The Certified Professional Secretary and Certified Administrative Professional are the international standards of measurement used to denote proficiency in the secretarial and administrative fields.

Certification can provide opportunities for career enhancement through job advancement, acquiring professional skills, salary increases, and self-esteem. In addition, many colleges and universities offer course credit for studying for and passing the CPS and CAP exams.

Both the CPS and CAP examinations are administered twice a year on consecutive weekends in May and November. Testing centers are located throughout the United States and Canada, as well as around the world. To qualify for either exam, applicants must meet the following criteria:

- Bachelor's degree and two years' administrative experience
- Associate degree and three years' administrative experience
- No degree and four years' administrative experience

Applicants for the CAP exam must have all experience completed and verified at the time they submit their application. CPS exam applicants may apply prior to completing all experience requirements, as long as they are currently employed in an administrative position or are a full-time student in a degree-granting program. CPS applicants have six years to complete the remaining experience, but the CPS rating will not be granted until all of the requirements are met.

The CPS exam is given in three parts and covers the following areas of administrative work:

- Office systems and technology
- Office administration
- Management

The CAP exam consists of four parts, which test candidates on the following areas:

- Office systems and technology
- Office administration
- Management
- Organizational management

The IAAP publishes a *Certification Review Guide* that includes exam outlines, sample questions, a bibliography of recommended study materials, and suggestions on exam review. The association strongly suggests that exam applicants use the review guide in their preparation for the tests.

Many employers have recognized the professionalism, broad range of knowledge, and upgraded skills achieved by certified secretaries. Many firms encourage secretaries to enroll in the CPS program by offering company reimbursement programs for tuition fees, textbooks, preparatory courses, and examination charges; others offer a monetary bonus and awards. Some give priority for managerial positions to certified secretaries, and others give a salary increase or a one-grade promotion. CPS holders earn an average of

$2,228 per year more than office professionals without it, according to the 2006 IAAP membership profile.

Because of the difficulty of the examination, secretaries who plan on taking it devote many hours or even years to preparing for it. Some colleges give credit for passing this examination and encourage certified professional secretaries to complete their formal education. Each college establishes its own criteria for awarding degree credit.

Information on the CPS and CAP examinations, applications, study materials, and testing centers is available from the IAAP at www.iaap-hq.org.

Professional Legal Secretary (PLS)

Certification as a professional legal secretary is available for lawyers' assistants who pass a one-day, four-part examination that demonstrates dedication to professionalism. The exam, administered by NALS, is open to those with three years of experience in the legal field. A partial waiver of the experience requirement may be granted for postsecondary degrees or other certifications.

The PLS exam is designed to certify a lawyer's assistant as a professional who possesses the following abilities:

- A mastery of office skills
- The ability to interact with attorneys, clients, and other support staff
- The discipline to assume responsibility and exercise initiative and judgment
- A working knowledge of procedural law, the law library, and how to prepare legal documents

The PLS exam is given in March and September of each year. All four parts of the test must be taken on the first attempt. If you do not pass all four parts, you may retake the parts that you failed. The exam covers the following areas:

1. Written communications
2. Office procedures and technology
3. Ethics and judgment
4. Legal knowledge and skills

Complete information about the PLS exam, testing locations, and study materials is available from NALS at www.nals.org.

Accredited Legal Secretary (ALS)

NALS developed this program for individuals at the apprentice level. To become accredited as a legal secretary, you must pass a four-hour, three-part examination that is offered four times a year: in March, June, September, and December. The three parts of the examination are the following:

1. Written communications
2. Office procedures and legal knowledge
3. Ethics, human relations, and judgment

Passing the examination will demonstrate the various skills that are required in a legal environment: perform business communication tasks, maintain office records and calendars, prioritize multiple tasks, understand office equipment and procedures, know legal terminology and document preparation, solve accounting problems, and follow law office protocol as prescribed by ethical codes.

Certified Medical Assistant (CMA)

The medical secretary can strive to achieve the certified medical assistant designation that certifies professional competence of individuals. The exam is sponsored by the American Association of Medical Assistants in cooperation with the National Board of Medical Examiners, which serves as an educational test consultant. It is given twice yearly at many test centers nationwide.

To qualify for the exam, you must graduate from a medical assisting program accredited by the Commission on Accreditation of Allied Health Education Programs (CAAHEP) or the Accrediting Bureau of Health Education Schools (ABHES). In addition, you must meet one of the following criteria:

- Graduating student or recent graduate of a CAAHEP-accredited medical assisting program
- Nonrecent graduate of a CAAHEP-accredited medical assisting program
- Graduating student or graduate of an ABHES-accredited medical assisting program

The AAMA has compiled a list of study materials for the exam. There is also a CMA exam review course offered at certain accredited medical assisting programs and local chapters of the AAMA. In addition, the booklet *A Candidate's Guide to the AAMA CMA Certification/Recertification Examination* includes a practice test.

Complete information about the certification process is available from the AAMA at www.aama-ntl.org.

9

PROMOTIONAL OPPORTUNITIES
FOR ADMINISTRATIVE ASSISTANTS

THIS IS AN opportune time for today's administrative assistants, who have acquired managerial skills and knowledge after assuming responsibilities formerly held by managers before downsizing and middle management layoffs began, to be promoted into middle managerial and professional levels. Statistics show that the percentage of managers in the workforce is on the rise, and the work they perform continues to evolve, as they act as coach, team leader, hand-holder, and overseer of projects. Opportunities that will provide potential career paths available to secretaries and administrative support personnel are related to desktop publishing, the Internet, and customer service support functions of organizations.

Secretaries who perceive themselves as professionals are career-oriented individuals who have set specific goals. They do not perceive their positions as dead-end jobs. Rather, in their pursuit of achieving designated targets, they direct all activities, both in and out of the office, toward this effort. They continually strive to strengthen their personal and professional qualifications. These individuals differ from secretaries who are content to remain in their own little niche, performing the tasks typically assigned to them, no more and no less. Career-oriented administrative assistants are intellectually active, innovative, and willing to do more than is required. They frequently strive for accreditation to improve in their profession and constantly seek ways to better themselves.

Advancement happens when workers plan strategies that include maximizing all work experiences, enrolling in continuing education courses, participating in workshops and seminars, reading extensively of the professional literature, joining professional and community organizations, taking leadership roles in associations, being aware of societal needs, and being knowledgeable about economic trends.

Generally, supervisory and managerial personnel advanced to a promotion in one or more steps. Becoming a supervisor of administrative assistants and other office personnel is the first step in the career ladder that involves planning, organizing, leading, and control. It is a position of responsibility and authority, one that places emphasis on managing human resources. The special skills a supervisor needs to manage others include personal attributes, creativity, an understanding of the factors that affect trends in the labor force, a knowledge and familiarity with changing technology, and the ability to influence workers and to gain their full support in carrying out the goals of the organization.

In this chapter, you will become familiar with the personal qualities and competencies needed for administrative advancement as well as the paths you can follow to achieve your goals.

Personal Qualities

Administrative assistants work in varied environments, probably no two exactly alike. They perform a multitude of tasks, some requiring much decision making.

Office automation has reduced the static nature of some secretarial jobs and has converted them into dynamic careers with unlimited promotional opportunities for forward-looking, ambitious, qualified individuals. In these environments, higher-level personal qualities are required for success and advancement. Employers look for good customer service and interpersonal skills because secretaries and administrative assistants must be tactful in their dealings with people. Discretion, good judgment, organizational or management ability, initiative, and the ability to work independently are especially important for higher-level administrative positions.

The National Organization of Colleges and Employers annual job outlook survey lists the top ten qualities/skills that employers look for in job candidates. In order of importance, they are:

1. Communication skills (verbal and written)
2. Honesty/integrity
3. Teamwork skills
4. Interpersonal skills
5. Motivation/initiative
6. Strong work ethic
7. Analytical skills
8. Flexibility/adaptability
9. Computer skills
10. Organizational skills

These characteristics indicate that an administrative assistant is a highly qualified employee who possesses not only a mastery of office skills but also personality requisites of the highest order. A further look at the help-wanted ads supports this concept of higher-order traits. Some frequently used adjectives and phrases to describe the kind of administrative assistant needed are: articulate, personable, self-confident, dynamic, bright, hard-working, unflappable in deadline-paced office, and flexible team worker. The secretary who possesses the qualities just enumerated usually gets ahead and eventually occupies a position of influence and status.

In addition to what employers are looking for, employees must be able to derive satisfaction from the job. The variety and level of tasks performed by the office professional directly influence job satisfaction, a human need that motivates individuals to achieve to the maximum of their abilities. Job satisfaction usually means happiness with the job, and, therefore, a more pleasing personality.

The ability to work as part of a team is increasingly important in today's workplace and will continue to be so in the office of the future. Researchers at Cornell University have found that the once desirable private office is no longer considered the best or most effective. A survey of 229 professionals at eight small firms found younger workers in particular preferred team-oriented offices because they offered greater access to colleagues from whom young workers felt they could learn. The consensus of the group was that the worst and least-effective office space is the Dilbert-style cubicle. Those surveyed felt that open offices are best because they foster more communication, cohesiveness, and learning without undermining ability to concentrate.[1]

----

1. Cornell University. "That's It on Dilbert Cubicles: The Workplace." *Work and Family Newsbrief,* June 2002.

Research tells us that one of the most important competencies for an administrative assistant is the ability to maintain good human relations. Personnel who have pleasing personalities, are courteous, and are cooperative usually function more successfully in the open-plan office designs where there is greater interaction among employees. These are also valuable qualities for harmonious working relationships in team projects. Frequently, when considering job mobility, many employers rank personal traits of congeniality, dependability, dedication, discretion, and self-assertiveness as important as skills and knowledge.

If your main goal is to achieve a managerial position, you should concentrate on developing interpersonal relations skills; flexibility in dealing with others and in making efficient changes in operations and procedures; willingness to delegate; ability to direct, guide, and motivate employees; projecting a pleasant, yet assertive personality and an enthusiastic and positive attitude; and understanding the company, including its goals, its policies, and its philosophies.

Professional Skills

An important part of exploring administrative careers is to carefully investigate the functions of positions and the skills and knowledge needed to fulfill the duties and responsibilities of the job. Also, be certain to identify the higher-level skills of supervisors and managers, information that you can use to determine how you can improve your own skills.

These employers are looking for well-rounded employees who have good interpersonal skills, can act efficiently and effectively in the workplace, and can ask pertinent questions. The professional skills that employers seek, taken from the Education and Professional Development Department of the IAAP[2] are listed below.

1. Project management
2. Software trainer (especially for executives and new hires)
3. Software adaptor (adapting software to specific company needs)
4. Website maintenance
5. Negotiation (with clients and vendors)
6. Online purchasing
7. Review and evaluation of furnishings and technology equipment (including phone systems, copiers, and so forth, for purchasing or leasing)
8. Coordination of mass mailings (including dealing with printers to determine the most cost-efficient methods to use)
9. Storage and retrieval of information (including e-info, tapes, videos, paper, multiformats, and so forth)
10. Scheduling and maintenance of calendars for self and others (mostly done electronically; also includes scheduling facilities)
11. Planning meetings (including negotiating hotel contracts, scheduling catering, preparing for cyber- and videoconferencing)
12. Planning travel (including online research, booking, tracking, preparing the traveler, securing needed information such as maps, alternatives, and so forth)

---

2. IAAP. Advanced Skills Admins Need to Excel in Today's Workplace. http://www.iaap hq.org/researchtrends/advanced_skills _admins_need_to_excel.htm, July 26, 2006.

13. Desktop publishing (brochures, flyers, annual reports)
14. Team leadership dealing with virtual members (from other facilities, traveling executives, or outside business partners)

To be considered an outstanding employee, you need to develop all of the above skills, accept challenges, have a positive attitude in life and work, assess your strengths and weaknesses, and continue learning by attending conventions, seminars, and workshops. Believe in yourself and strive to reach your goals.

To get ahead in the administrative professions, individuals who have broad skills and knowledge in information processing and who have the necessary administrative ability will be most likely to reach higher levels of responsibility in either supervisory or managerial positions.

Paths to Professional Growth

Professional growth is the key to career satisfaction. As you become involved in activities that lead to self-improvement, you become not only more valuable to your employer but a potential candidate for promotion. To realize your maximum level of abilities, you should avail yourself of every opportunity that will further develop you personally as well as your skills and knowledge. Here are some suggestions for growing professionally.

• Join professional organizations whose membership consists of supervisory and managerial personnel or some other business-related group. The contacts you make in other business areas will help to broaden your experience and provide you with good contacts for the future. During organizational meetings or seminars, you will have opportunities to share ideas with other interested members.

• Become involved in organizational projects that develop leadership skills.

• Volunteer your services in your area of expertise.

• Assume jobs that will give you high visibility.

• Find a mentor, a high-level manager or executive who can advise and guide you. In reaching your goals, this person may also recommend you to the "right" contacts.

• Listen attentively to what others are saying.

• Become a specialist in a particular area, such as personnel evaluation.

• Visit equipment exhibitors and attend seminars.

• Read professional literature, such as *Executive Secretary and Administrative Assistant, Corporate Secretary, Working Woman,* and *Administrative Professional Update.*

• Seek accreditation in a profession other than secretarial, such as Certified Administrative Manager (CAM).

Professional Organizations

You can make important contacts through memberships in professional organizations. Companies frequently pay membership dues for employees who join professional organizations and reimburse them for costs incurred when attending meetings and conferences. Both company and employee benefit—the worker in terms of personal and professional growth, the company in terms of visibility and contribution to the educational process.

As an active member, you meet other individuals with similar or related interests. You also have opportunities to develop your communication and leadership skills by joining committees formed for specific tasks. From presenters at meetings who share some of their expertise with you, you broaden your horizons and learn a great deal.

To gain the broadest possible knowledge, you should consider joining organizations in areas other than strictly administrative. You will not only add to your knowledge base but will also begin to gain visibility in the business community. From participation in seminars and conventions, you will also gain many ideas that in turn will help you become more creative. Your association with other professionals will enhance your professional growth in terms of knowledge, understanding of trends in business, and managerial concepts.

See Chapter 8 for descriptions of some specialized secretarial organizations, their activities, and their purposes. All of these organizations have local chapters that you ought to investigate about membership.

Company Training Programs

Society will continue to experience greater changes during this decade than it has in the past. New job categories will emerge, job requirements will change, the way in which work is performed will vary, and where work is done will change. Companies are beginning to realize that people have become the major asset of a business enterprise; therefore, training is a critical element in a firm's operations.

As automated systems are updated, it is necessary to train employees to operate the sophisticated equipment and to learn the new procedures. Educational training programs are not new in corporate training departments. Through the years, trainers have been designing and scheduling courses offered either during company hours or after working hours. Generally, these programs are established to:

- Orient employees to company procedures
- Train employees on new equipment
- Provide opportunities for additional learning relevant to company activities
- Provide employees with job enrichment as well as new jobs and responsibilities
- Develop basic and advanced skills in areas such as English, writing, and software programs
- Provide remediation for those who demonstrate a need
- Learn new skills and knowledge for upward mobility
- Prepare for career switching

Many companies offer structured training in the form of in-service programs, which consist of three basic types:

1. **On-the-job training.** Beginning workers are trained at their workstations under the supervision of an experienced employee.

2. **Vestibule training (usually conducted by larger firms).** Training is given away from the work area but usually during working hours. Instruction is provided with generally the same equipment, materials, and procedures as pertain to the actual job in an on-site classroom. The objectives of this training are to raise levels of employees' skills, to orient them to company procedures, and to teach advanced skills for promotional opportunities.

3. **After-hours or off-premises training.** This is training taken voluntarily by employees for personal development.

Tuition-Reimbursement Programs

Many companies with training plans allow employees to enroll in college or university courses. For example, in tuition-refund plans, personnel enroll in undergraduate or graduate courses in local colleges or in continuing education classes, which have been one of the fastest-growing educational areas. The adult segment of the population usually registers in continuing education courses to update skills, as a refresher, or for professional development.

Payment for education outside company programs falls under two general categories: partial or full reimbursement. Policies vary greatly from firm to firm, some requiring that the course be job-related and others that a grade of C or better be earned. Some companies reimburse employees based on actual grade received; others pay a stipulated amount for a course at a college and a lesser sum for a course at a nonaccredited institution or professional school. Still other institutions share the tuition and registration expenses. Many companies, however, do reimburse employees for total course expenditures if completed successfully.

The bottom line of continuing education is professional growth with the potential for upward mobility. Company training programs are usually beneficial to both employee and employer in terms of productivity, loyalty, skills, and knowledge.

Networking

Building personal and professional relationships is important, and a network is the vehicle through which you will be exposed to contacts and information that will help you grow. When you network, you are developing contacts with individuals who might be helpful in your career. There are numerous ways in all industries for employees to become acquainted. They may know of potential openings or may know of somebody else to whom they can introduce you. Research indicates that leads are one of the most effective ways of finding out about a job. In addition to being helpful in your job search, these individuals can lend emotional support. To benefit from such a group, you should abide by the following principles and strategies.

- Join and become active in a professional association.
- Become involved with a civic, social, or religious organization.
- Keep organized records of contacts—names, addresses, and telephone numbers.
- Be a good listener, ask questions, and show interest.
- Give as well as receive information.
- Lend someone a helping hand.
- Make a point of talking to your supervisors and coworkers on a regular basis if you are a telecommuter.
- Build confidence by assessing your strengths.
- Show respect to others.
- Be aware of what is happening in your firm and in the field.

Networking, according to the literature, should help you believe in yourself, which is the first step toward success. This technique has been widely adopted by men and women alike in many occupations all over the country. Make certain that your contact network grows and does not shrink. Be optimistic, pleasant, and lively when with other people. These characteristics are attractive to others and help build relationships.

10

The Job Search in the Information Age

"It's not the best-prepared student who gets the job, but the student who is best prepared at getting the job," is a statement that gets right to the point when you are looking for employment. There are many ways in which to hunt for a job; however, initially you should do some research on the workplace to gain an understanding of the latest trends both in the office environment and competition in the workforce.

You have read in this book about many options within the administrative field. As you begin to search for employment, you will find that you have many decisions to make as to the kind of firm you would like to work for, where you would like to live, whether you work better on your own or as part of a group, whether a particular industry or profession is more compatible with your interests and abilities, and whether you prefer a large automated office or a small traditional-type environment. The first job you accept has a very important influence on you. This is your first work experience in your chosen profession, and it shapes your attitudes about the career.

The career you choose should unlock your potential for achievement on the job and bring about personal growth. This can only occur when your goals, skills, knowledge, and ambitions are matched to the job you select. You should take a personal inventory to determine your interests, strengths, and weaknesses, factors that should be considered in the selection of a job that will enable you to progress into more responsible positions. Above all, choose a job where the atmosphere and pace are comfortable for you and where the job responsibilities are compatible with your abilities.

This chapter will prepare you to make decisions about your initial position and plan your strategies for your job search.

Location

The growing number of professional centers and business complexes being constructed in the suburbs give administrative assistants the choice of working close to home or traveling. Generally, salaries are higher in cities than in suburban districts; however, depending on your values and needs, each location has particular advantages.

Main offices of banks, stores, and government agencies, as well as executive offices and showrooms of large corporations, are usually found in cities. In these metropolitan areas, employees have the benefit of cultural opportunities that generally are not available in suburban areas. The atmosphere is usually more sophisticated; there is greater emphasis on dress code; and more money is spent on food, entertainment, and clothing. In suburban districts, dress is more casual and living expenses are lower.

You have to determine whether you would prefer to work in the fast-paced, more crowded environment of a city or the quieter surroundings of a suburban area. Depending on where you live and plan to work, you also need to consider what your daily commute will involve. The growing number of people who choose to live in the suburbs and work in the city face a daily commute of sometimes more than two hours each way. Would you prefer a short bus or train ride to work, or perhaps an hour-long commute by train or car? Be sure to factor in the expenses of commuting when determining your needs.

Type and Size of Office

If you have special interests in music, art, or medicine, which for various reasons you could not pursue as a career field, you might wish to find a job in an industry related to them. For example, a person who is interested in music might choose to work with a publisher of musical scores; in art, with a museum; and in medicine, with a hospital or medical school. Keep in mind that the most satisfying career for you will be the one that is in harmony with your interests.

In a small office you will have opportunities to perform a multitude of tasks. However, no matter how skillfully you perform your duties, there is very little room for advancement. Jobs are available in offices of private doctors, dentists, lawyers, and engineers; in real estate offices; and in branch offices of banks and insurance companies. The atmosphere is usually less rigid and more informal than in a large company that employs hundreds of workers. Although working hours are regulated, the administrative assistant in a smaller office generally has more freedom to change work schedules. Depending on where you work, public transportation may or may not be available; however, employees usually drive to work where parking space is provided. A disadvantage is that salaries are more related to a company's fixed budget rather than your competence.

In large offices, the environment is more structured, lines of authority are clearly defined, and personnel policies are set. Work is specialized based on departmental structure. In a more or less traditional setting, the executive secretary who works on a one-to-one basis for the president or another major executive may handle all the administrative details of mail, e-mail, faxing, record keeping, appointments, correspondence, meetings, and the like. In an automated environment that is fully equipped with the latest office technology and systems, the secretary/administrative assistant/office professional usually supports several managers in the organization and has a very wide range of responsibilities, including managerial and administrative duties. This employee generally has good technical skills, both oral and written communication skills, and a personality and personal attributes that make a good team player. No matter in which size office you prefer to work, remember that you must always be ready to learn and to remain in a learning mode, for changes continue to occur very quickly. The skills you have today might be outmoded in a few months, and so the job will change.

Opportunities for advancement to supervisory and managerial positions exist as well as lateral movement to positions in other departments. Other advantages of working for a large firm are the benefits, which can include company training programs and tuition-reimbursement plans, company-subsidized cafeterias, bonuses, scholarships for children of employees, daycare centers, credit unions, stock-buying privileges, group life insurance, medical benefits, hospitalization, and dental insurance. Frequently, the spouse and children under nineteen years of age who are living at home are included in medical insurance plans. These fringe benefits account for approximately 40 percent of company personnel expenses, not including payment of salaries.

Conducting the Job Search

After you have identified the secretarial career that you wish to pursue and for which you feel most qualified, determine the geographic area where you would like to work. Then identify companies where you would like to work and where you anticipate openings will occur from downsizing in middle management, growth, or turnover and replacement. If you are uncertain as to where to concentrate your efforts, try to find data on industries that have the best overall employment prospects.

Plan your job search strategies according to the following steps:

• Develop a network of personal contacts.
• Compile a list of target companies and do some research to find out about their products or services, status in the industry, size, growth potential, information about the job in which you're interested, and the person who would hire you. Call each company for an annual report and available literature on the firm.
• Use the Internet for your search. There are thousands of jobs listed on the Internet, and the Web has many electronic career cen-

ters that offer information of all types, including job listings. Sites such as monster.com and careerbuilder.com list thousands of positions and provide résumé-building services.

- Develop your résumé.
- Write a letter of application.
- Strengthen your interviewing skills and maintain records of interviews.
- Send thank-you letters.

Although Internet job searches are very productive, you should also continue to use the traditional ways to find a job: newspapers and journals, contacts, and agencies. Most important, you must develop a job prospect list. This list should include friends, relatives, instructors, employers, key people in organizations, school placement offices, newspaper advertisements, employment agencies, company recruiters, and company personnel offices.

Friends, Relatives, and Instructors

Let friends and relatives know that you are looking for a job. Discuss your goals with them and ask them to tell you if a position becomes available in their company or elsewhere. You might ask them to call other acquaintances who might know of openings. Sometimes opportunities come from casual conversation, and someone you know might be aware of a job that would appeal to you.

School Placement Offices

Both high school and college placement offices receive listings of job openings. They also have counselors available to advise students; these counselors can help you prepare a résumé and tell you about part-time and summer employment in addition to full-time work. They may also be able to make good suggestions for interviewing, particularly if they know something about a particular firm.

It is advisable to file a portfolio with the placement office. The file should contain recommendations from teachers, a personal data sheet, and other credentials. Keep this information current so that your employment status is up to date. Executive recruiters who come to the colleges to interview students examine this portfolio.

Advertisements in Newspapers and Professional Magazines

Reading these ads regularly will help you to learn what kinds of employees are needed, where openings are available, and what skills are needed. You will also gain insight into salaries offered, and even benefits. These advertisements will have either a company name and address or will be a "blind" ad, whereby you respond to a box number or a telephone number. Blind ads are placed to eliminate unqualified applicants.

Answer an ad promptly in whichever manner of application is specified, whether it is a letter of application and a résumé, or an electronic application. Read ads carefully for any desired qualities that are mentioned, such as "savvy and poise," "high-voltage person with grasp of detail," "ambitious," "highly organized," "good phone personality," "knowledge of Word," and "computer literate." Also check to see if anything in the ad makes this company unique, such as a four-day workweek or flexible hours.

Employment Agencies

There are two types of employment agencies: public and private. You may register without a fee at a public employment agency by completing an application form, taking an English test and computer skills test, and being interviewed. Many state agencies are tied into a job-bank program, where openings are fed into a computer and where a printout is available to anyone who wants it. The state employment agencies are linked together in a network by the U.S. Employment Service.

Private employment agencies charge a fee, usually paid by the employer. They have many leads to good jobs, but use these firms with caution. The jobs that sound great in the ads aren't always available when you get there. Also, guard against being swayed by them to take a job that may not be exactly the kind you want. Be sure to register with several agencies that serve your field of work. Private agencies service the companies by doing the preliminary screening, testing, and interviewing. Only applicants with the qualifications for the job are sent to the company seeking help. These agencies range in size and some of them cater to certain skill areas or fields of work.

Refer to the section on "Temporary Employment" in Chapter 4 where outsourcing is discussed. You may want to sign up with this type of agency, too.

Government Service

There are hundreds of thousands of administrative openings in civil service each year in cities and towns throughout the nation as well as in foreign countries. All except a few of these jobs require a competitive examination before appointment. Test results are entered on a list in ranked order of scores. Books written specifically for civil service exams are available in local bookstores and can help you prepare for these tests. To be eligible for U.S. appointments, an applicant must be a citizen of the United States or Canada and must meet the minimum age, training, and experience requirements for the position.

The official job site of the U.S. federal government is www .usajobs.com. You can search for federal positions throughout the United States and around the world and can apply online for most jobs. In Canada, visit www.jobs-emplois.gc.ca for access to federal job information.

Job Searching on the Internet

There are a number of advantages to using the Internet in your job search, aside from the number and diversity of jobs you can find there.

- You may be able to delve into the hidden job market, which is the world of unadvertised openings.
- Many major corporations list job openings on websites because employers can fill jobs faster and less expensively.
- You can send your résumé to local firms as well as those across the country.
- You can find lists of jobs organized in many categories, such as state, occupation, industry, or part-time/full-time.
- A search can be done at any hour of the day and doesn't interfere with a work schedule.
- Information can be found on the interview process and type of questions asked.

Other Sources

You may apply directly to companies for which you would like to work by sending a letter of application and a résumé. Your letter should indicate that you will call to determine if a position is available. This call or correspondence might reach the company at an opportune time for you, perhaps just as a job is about to be advertised. Using this technique will help you to be viewed as someone with initiative and drive.

You may also apply directly to a business by walking into a human resources department and filing an application. If there are no openings at the time, your credentials will be filed for later reference; however, it is wise to follow up with an occasional call.

Contact as many sources as you believe can help. Don't sit back and wait for things to happen. Conduct an active job campaign.

When you look for a job, you really have to sell yourself very much the way you would sell a product. In this instance, you are the product that you want to sell to a firm so that you can be hired for a specific job. To do so effectively, you must know yourself and evaluate yourself honestly. You sell yourself through a résumé, an application letter, and an interview. In each of these processes, you should remember to accentuate your strengths. Let the employer know that you are confident in your abilities to assume the responsibilities of the job.

The Application Letter

The application letter is the first step in securing a position, and it is sent usually in response to an advertisement for a job opening. Generally it is accompanied by a résumé. This letter should highlight aspects of your background that support your statement that you are the right person for the job.

Your letter is the very first impression you will be making on the recipient. It should be not only neat and visually attractive but an attention-getter, one that establishes a contact. An application letter usually has three parts:

1. The opening should create interest, state your purpose, and reveal where you learned of the position: "I believe that I have the maturity, creativity, and technical skills needed to be a successful administrative assistant, as advertised in today's *Los Angeles Times.*"

2. The body of the letter should contain convincing statements that show how your qualifications, education, and experience meet the employer's requirements. In this section, express a genuine interest in the company and make a positive statement why you would like to work for it: "I am impressed not only with your products but also with the many activities you support in this city. Working for your company, I know, would be a valuable learning experience." Or, "My work with the elderly, my background in psychology, and my excellent communication skills make me the very logical candidate for the job."

3. The closing paragraph should stimulate action by requesting an interview. Indicate that you will call at a particular time to arrange for this: "I would very much like to be interviewed for the position. I will call your office Thursday morning to speak with you about an appointment. If you wish to reach me before Thursday, my telephone number is 555-5555."

Résumés

A well-prepared résumé is a vital tool for job hunters. It highlights significant details of your history and indicates important personal data, career objectives, educational background, work experience, and special interests and accomplishments. A carefully prepared résumé should state just enough about your skills and abilities to impress the prospective employer. The time you spend in collecting, analyzing, preparing, and then recording the data will serve a twofold purpose: (1) to sell your qualifications as an employee to an employer, and (2) to prepare you for the interview. Once you have organized the data to reflect your strengths, you can then discuss these items with assurance.

The Traditional Résumé

Traditional résumés are written in a style that gets the reader's attention. This is usually achieved by creativity in expression and use of action verbs, bolding, underlining, bullets, and colored paper. One type is the reverse chronological résumé, which lists the dates of employment and educational background in reverse chronological order. (See Figure 10.1.) The functional format emphasizes skills and accomplishments as they relate to the job for which you are applying. This format stresses your strengths and skill groupings, but it presents your employment history in less detail than does the chronological résumé. (See Figure 10.2.)

Make your résumé unique. You want it to stand out among all those submitted by your competitors. One way to accomplish this is to have it printed on a textured beige- or ivory-colored paper. To enhance the appearance of your résumé, arrange it skillfully by using wide margins and side headings; keep narrative to one side, properly aligned.

Try to keep your résumé to one page, which shouldn't be difficult if you are a student with limited work experience. If you have had extensive experience, advanced education, or significant achievements, then add a second page if necessary, but try to be as succinct as possible.

Figure 10.1 Sample Traditional Résumé

Amanda Weaver

2896 Wellman Avenue

East Greenwich, RI 02215

(401) 555-9103

aweaver@abc.net

Career Objective

To perform responsibilities of an administrative manager in a secretarial support
environment in a legal department

Education

Community College of Rhode Island

West Warwick, RI 02889

A.A.S. Degree

Field of Study: Secretarial and Office Systems, Legal Option

Related Courses

Law Office Management   Business Law

Introduction to Accounting Legal Procedures

Introduction to Psychology

Secretarial Skills

Keying: 65 wpm

Shorthand: 120 wpm

Machine Skills: transcriber, personal computer, scanner

Software Programs: WordPerfect Office X3, Lotus Domino Document Manager,

Powerpoint, Photoshop

continued

Figure 10.1 Sample Traditional Résumé *continued*

Other Skills

Reading, writing, and conversational fluency in Spanish

Awards and Honors

Certificate for dean's list earned during Fall 2004, Spring 2005, Fall 2005, and Spring 2006

Work Experience

Spring 2005

Management Internship Training Program

Community College of Rhode Island

Duties: Assisted secretary to dean of college, typed correspondence and reports, and handled the telephone

Summer 2006

Lambert and Morales

Title: Legal Secretary

127 Eddy Street

Providence, RI 02912

Duties: Took dictation in shorthand, answered the telephone, maintained the calendar, transcribed recorded dictation, and inputted legal documents such as wills and agreements on an desktop computer

References

Furnished on request

Figure 10.2 Sample Functional Résumé

Amanda Weaver

2896 Wellman Avenue

East Greenwich, RI 02215

(401) 555-9103

aweaver@abc.net

Career Objective: To perform responsibilities of an administrative manager in a secretarial support environment in a legal department

Special Qualifications: Three years of experience with increasing responsibilities in addition to thirty credits earned toward a B.A. degree in office systems

Work Experience:

Administrative Assistant—Worked for three managers of Warren Industries, Palm Springs, CA; set up a filing system for the department; supervised the general clerks; coordinated joint meetings held by senior and junior partners; scheduled appointments with clients

Executive Secretary—Was secretary to one of the vice presidents of a major textile organization; supervised the secretarial staff; performed general administrative assignments; handled confidential files; typed general and legal documents; transcribed legal documents

Memberships: International Association of Administrative Professionals
National Association of Legal Secretaries

References: Provided upon request

As you begin to accumulate pertinent data, develop an asset list under the headings: personal data, career objectives, educational background, work experience, special interests and affiliations, and references. After you have gathered these data, discard those items that aren't relevant to secretarial positions and include everything you believe the employer would be interested in knowing about you. A brief description of each section of the résumé follows:

• **Personal data.** Every résumé must include your name, address, and telephone number. You should also include your cellular phone number and e-mail address. Federal legislation limits inquiries about age, sex, and marital status, information that should not be included on your résumé. Any other personal information, such as race or religious affiliation, should also be omitted.

• **Career objective.** An effective résumé should have a specific career focus. You may indicate the position you would seek after a period of time at this company. Be specific in your statement: "To perform as an administrative assistant to an executive in charge of marketing operations where there are opportunities for professional growth."

• **Education.** If you have a college degree, then it isn't necessary to include high school background. Under this category, include date of graduation, degree or professional certificate earned, major, and courses related to your career choice. Special projects that contributed to your professional development should be included.

In this category, elaborate on the level of skills you have with equipment as well as any language fluency.

Usually special honors, awards, or scholarships are earned during the time you are attending school. These items reflect a good image of you and should become part of your résumé.

• **Work experience.** Undoubtedly, prospective employers will read this section carefully to determine if your experience relates to the company's needs. Include internships and cooperative work experience programs. Highlight significant data and use action verbs, such as *developed, managed,* and *headed* to describe the work you have done.

Use reverse chronological order to list your experience—that is, list your most recent job first. Include title of job and major duties performed.

A few words of caution! Do not leave time gaps under the topic headings in your résumé. This might lead an employer to incorrect assumptions.

• **Special interests and affiliations.** Your special interests, hobbies, and extracurricular activities also might give the employer an idea about you. For example, holding an office in a professional organization would show leadership abilities. Involvement in community programs might reflect ability to interact with others.

• **References.** References need not be included on the résumé. You may simply state, "References will be furnished on request." When you submit names of individuals as references, select those persons who can speak with authority on your performance, such as employers, instructors, and administrators. Do not give the names of friends or relatives. Before you use an individual's name for reference, obtain permission to do so. You might develop a list of names as references so that you can be selective and suggest different people for different positions.

There are several acceptable styles for preparing a résumé. You may wish to use the sample résumés in this chapter as a guide for formatting your own.

The Electronic Résumé

To keep up with the job market, you need to be able to produce an electronic résumé that can easily be searched and scanned by the computer. For your résumé to be searchable, you must use keywords or nouns for database searching, not action words. Many companies that advertise job openings request that résumés are sent electronically rather than by mail or fax. Recruiters also check online résumé databases to find candidates for unadvertised job openings. With the right software, employers can now compare the résumés of hundreds of applicants for a job.

One of the most popular formats to use when keying an electronic résumé for e-mail is the plain text style, which the majority of firms can accept. Avoid italics, underlining, different font sizes, graphics, and lines. The computer will read circles as the letter "O"; use solid dots or bullets. To highlight something, use either capital letters, dashes, or asterisks. Another important technique is to make certain a line has no more than sixty-five characters because it cannot be recognized by the computer. Always test the résumé for clarity by sending it to yourself before sending it to a company. (See Figure 10.3.)

When you post your résumé on an online database, you are receiving very wide exposure and marketing yourself worldwide. This is a good method to use if you plan to relocate to another city or country.

The Job Interview

The interview is the last and one of the most important steps in being hired for a position. This is your opportunity to sell yourself and to demonstrate that you are the best candidate for the job. This

Figure 10.3 Sample Electronic Résumé

Amanda Weaver
2896 Wellman Avenue
East Greenwich, RI 02215
(401) 555-9103
aweaver@abc.net

Keywords: Management internship, legal office, Spanish, take dictation in short-hand, assisted secretary to dean; type, business law, accounting, computer, dean's list, shorthand, Word Perfect Office X3, Lotus Domino Document Manager, Excel, Powerpoint; telephone.

Skills: Key 65 wpm, shorthand 120 wpm, transcribe recorded dictation, key legal documents, computer skills, use variety of software, schedule appointments

Employment History:
1. Management Internship Training Program at Lakeville Community College, 2005
Assisted secretary to dean; typed correspondence/reports; handled the telephone

2. Legal Secretary, Lambert & Morales, 2006
Took dictation in shorthand; answered telephone; maintained calendar;
Inputted legal documents such as wills and agreements

Education: A.A.S. Degree
Community College of Rhode Island
West Warwick, RI

Professional Organizations:
National Association of Legal Secretaries
International Association of Administrative Professionals

is the first time the employer gets a personal impression of you as an individual and as a prospective employee. Interviews are given in several different ways: telephone, computer, Internet, or face-to-face.

The telephone interview is often the first contact an applicant has with a potential employer. The purpose is to get an understanding of the person's background to determine his or her suitability for the job. Either a manager from the firm who has the responsibility of hiring or a human resources person asks the applicant a series of questions. If the candidate makes a good impression and has the right qualifications for the job, the firm's representative will set a date for a face-to-face interview.

The computerized job interview is now being used by many companies instead of the traditional screening interview. In this situation, the computer asks the questions of the applicants about their background, work experience, and skills. When this system was first developed, the interview consisted of multiple-choice and true/false questions. However, some systems now have questions that require written responses. All questions are customized for relevancy to each company and the position that is open. The interviewer accesses from the computer a summary of the applicant's responses. This might lead to a face-to-face interview. Of interest to you are the special computers with lenses that transmit head-and-shoulder images of the recruiter and interviewee when conducting face-to-face interviews in corporate offices and campus centers.

The Internet job interview is used for initial screening. The applicant is given the password to get access to the company's computer system. After logging on, the applicant is asked the usual questions about background, work experience, and skills.

The face-to-face interview conducted in the office environment is the last chance for you to make an impression and determine if you are interested in the position. The interview is a two-way communication process during which unsuitable applicants are screened out. You should plan for this interview so that the experience can be beneficial to you. Some guidelines you might pursue before you go on an interview are: researching the company; evaluating your career goals, values, likes, dislikes, strengths, and weaknesses; dressing appropriately; being yourself; anticipating questions; and preparing supplies.

Researching the Company

Before the interview, you should gather as much information as possible about the company, its products and services, its potential for growth, the department and opening for which you are being interviewed, and its reputation in terms of employer/employee relations and community activities. You need to know something about the organization so that you can determine how you can be an asset to it. In addition, your knowledge about the company and comments reflecting how you can contribute to its operations surely will impress the interviewer.

There are several methods for learning about a company. First, try to get the name and title of the person who will interview you. Then read all you can about the company in its annual report, in its recruiting brochures, in its publications or website, and in its product news releases. You might call the public relations department of the company and ask for its literature. If you secured this interview from an employment agency, then ask the agency for some insight into the company. Another alternative is to check library reference books and business publications such as those put out by Dun and Bradstreet and Standard & Poor's. You might even call a stockbroker. Finally, read the advertisements in the newspapers.

Information on small firms may be gathered from the local chamber of commerce.

Evaluating Your Career Goals

You should take stock of yourself, what you want in a career, your motivation to achieve, and what you have accomplished in previous jobs that demonstrates marketable skills and productivity. Think about your likes and dislikes and whether your interests match your skills and abilities. Finding out about yourself will help you recognize your own potential. This will enable you to speak with self-confidence about yourself, your interests, and what you have to offer.

Dressing Appropriately

Dress conservatively on the day of the interview. Women should avoid excessive jewelry and makeup. Avoid extreme hairstyles. A skirt and blouse, tailored dress, or suit is appropriate. Men should be clean-shaven and dressed in business attire. Jeans will not make a good impression.

Being Yourself

You need to be happy working for a company; and, therefore, you ought to be accepted as you really are. However, sometimes it is necessary to modify behavior. For example, you must be friendly, casual, courteous, and professional. Most important, be honest. Remember, the requirements of the job should be matched with a person's talents, desires, and abilities so that both company and employee benefit. The key to a successful interview lies in your ability to convey a positive attitude about yourself.

Anticipating Questions

If you anticipate some questions that the interviewer might ask and think about your responses, you might relieve some of your tensions. The interviewer generally is trying to determine your self-confidence, whether your career goals are defined, and your degree of interest and enthusiasm for the position. In addition, your level of maturity, self-assertiveness, intelligence, and results orientation are also being evaluated.

Questions may be either open-ended or structured, in which the interviewer seeks specific information. There will probably be some "ice-breakers," questions that are intended to put you at ease. Your answers to most of these will come from your self-assessment, which should reinforce how important it is to take the time to perform this valuable task.

Typical questions asked during interviews are:

What can you tell me about your personal background?
How would you describe yourself?
Why did you select a secretarial career?
What do you see yourself doing five years from now?
What approaches are you going to use to reach your
    ultimate career goals?
What are some of your major strengths?
What are your biggest weaknesses? (Use a strength to
    answer this and report it as a weakness. For example, if
    you like to get a job done without procrastinating, state

you are impatient at times because you like to get your
work out on schedule. Or you might indicate that you
are a perfectionist and that you will not release work
until it is perfect.)

What do you consider your greatest achievement?

What do you do when two priorities compete for your
time?

What skills do you have that you feel need strengthening?

Do you enjoy working alone or with other people? What
courses did you like best in school?

Your résumé shows several short-term jobs. Could you
explain?

Your résumé indicates several part-time positions while you
were going to school. Do you believe these work
experiences helped you as an individual? How?

Why did you leave your last job?

In selecting your career, did you consider the ease with
which you absorbed knowledge in certain subjects?
How?

Why should we consider you for the job? Usually we hire
someone with more experience than you have to offer.

How can you make a contribution to our company?

What do you know about our company?

Preparing Supplies

A few days before the scheduled interview, prepare a list of everything you must do or take with you. Assemble your social security
card, several copies of your résumé, a list of references, several pens
and sharpened pencils, a school transcript, and any personal work

you would like to show the interviewer. On an index card, you should list facts about the company. You might wish to refer to them during your trip to the interview. You should have questions for the interviewer. Jot them down on a card so that you don't fail to ask them; this shows interest and initiative.

The Application

When you come to the interview, you might be asked to complete an application form. Use the information from your résumé as you respond to the questions. Use a pen, write legibly, and respond to every question. If a question does not pertain to you, indicate that you read this question by responding with "NA," meaning "not applicable."

During the Interview

Interviewers begin to evaluate candidates for jobs from the moment they read application letters and résumés or conduct the interview, whichever is first. On written documents, interviewers look for appearance, arrangement, creativity in writing, initiative, and content. Since your résumé indicates your measurable skills and aptitudes, it will help the interviewer determine whether your skills meet the requirements of the position.

Equally important are the intangible skills and personal qualities that come across during the interview. How do you communicate ideas in speaking? Do you have your own opinions? Do you ask questions if you need clarification of a statement? Do you listen attentively? Do you establish eye contact? Do you communicate a positive attitude? Factors used to evaluate a prospective employee are personality, maturity, motivation, flexibility, and enthusiasm.

In secretarial careers, personal traits and qualifications are essential for success, especially in view of the constantly changing nature of the office, society, and business.

After the Interview

Be certain to thank the interviewer by name for having taken time to see you. If the interviewer doesn't indicate when a decision will be made, suggest that you will call on a certain day to find out if an applicant has been selected for the job.

Follow up the interview with a thank-you note in which you express your interest in the job and the opportunity to work for the company.

Each interview you have should be a learning experience and should lead to increased self-confidence. So don't fret if you don't get the job. Rather, think positively and apply what you learned from the first interview to the next one. Reassure yourself that you are the best-qualified candidate for the job.

You might wish to maintain a record of your contacts so that you don't make the mistake of responding to the same help-wanted advertisement more than once. A sample form you might develop is shown in Figure 10.4.

Once You Have a Job

You will want to keep your job search records on file, even after you have your job, because they represent an ongoing record of business contacts that you will enlarge and use many times during your career. Discard duplicate papers—you only need one good list

Figure 10.4 Record of Employer Contact

Company Name Address Phone E-mail	Application Letter Mailed	Résumé Mailed (Hard Copy or E-mail)	Interview Date (Phone, Computer, or Face-to-Face)	Interviewer	Thank-You Note Sent	Follow-Up Letter Sent	Offer Received	Rejection Received
Argo, Inc. 1 Olga Dr. Clifton, NJ 20363 201-555-5500 argo@zz.com	4/06	4/06	4/25	Donna Jones	4/26	5/10	5/11	

of the names and addresses and company titles—and keep your file orderly and updated. You might also want to keep your records in a spreadsheet.

Networking means developing business contacts that will keep you in touch with many segments of your industry. You will learn a great deal by becoming a member of professional associations and maintaining your contacts with people in your business field. You will also find that, as you gain experience, you'll have more and more opportunity to contribute to your field in a professional capacity. In the beginning, you can volunteer to help with simple tasks in your professional organization by doing mailings, gathering news for the monthly bulletin, or making phone calls for special campaigns. Later, as you learn more about your field, you may want to help with programs, lead panel discussions, report on changes in your industry, or hold an office.

Hints for Success in Your Career

The office workplace offers many more opportunities for a career with growth potential than ever before. It is up to you to make things happen. You must learn as much as you can about yourself, your needs, and your career goals, both short- and long-range.

You can gain insight about the administrative career path by reading the literature. The consensus on the following comments is clearly indicated: administrative assistants receive greater respect than ever before; organizations are relying more on management skills of administrative staff; secretaries are members of the management team; and more managerial duties are being delegated to secretaries. Below are some suggestions to open doors to upward mobility.

- Focus on the group's goals and objectives.
- Maintain a positive image.
- Use initiative, innovation, and creativity.
- Adopt a management frame of mind.
- Become cross-trained and learn as much as you can about your department.
- Make lifelong learning a goal through seminars, workshops, and college enrollment.
- Become a computer software expert.
- Be flexible and a good team player.
- Develop and focus on good interpersonal skills.
- Develop leadership qualities.
- Become a good organizer and know where and how to search for information needed to manage projects.

Administrative assistants say: "Well-trained admins who take their career seriously can reach for the stars." "Being a secretary is a dynamic career." "Practice being a 'people' person." Other qualities mentioned are the importance of a positive attitude, building a good rapport with the employer, polishing language skills, continuing one's education, adapting to change, and being willing to accept challenges.

Enriching Your Professional Life Is Up to You

There are endless possibilities, and you will discover more and more of these as you go along. Talk with the other people in the office where you get your job. Learn to be a good coworker, and a good friend by being tactful, useful, and reliable on the job. Your coworkers can be helpful in letting you know the expectations of the department, the office style in the little things like who usually takes care of social plans such as birthday lunches and holiday gift exchanges. These are small parts of each working day that you will want to participate in and enjoy with the rest of the office staff. They provide good opportunities for you to get to know the others and to hear from them in an informal way many of the other small details that make up the fabric of office life. By being a good listener, you will be able to learn a good deal that will help you get along well and make a place for yourself in the new group.

Continuing education, whether on-the-job or in a school evenings or weekends, plus the contacts at work and in professional associations will help to enrich your professional life. They will help to provide knowledge and contacts that will assist you when you consider a job change, promotion, or expansion of your duties. Administrative careers can carry you to a great variety of challenging roles in many kinds of work, and, with care, your career can be a satisfying, many-sided adventure.

About the Author

BLANCHE ETTINGER IS a professor in the Business Department at Bronx Community College of The City University of New York and a former adjunct professor in the Business Education Program at New York University. She initially taught on the high school level; prior to that she was secretary to the executive vice president of Cohn Hall Marx Company.

She received her B.A. degree and M.S. in education from Hunter College of The City University of New York and an Ed.D. in business education from New York University, where she also took many courses in guidance and occupational information.

Ettinger has earned a national reputation for her many contributions to the field of business education. Through the years, she has been active in professional organizations and has served as president of the Business Education Association of Metropolitan New York; New York State Association of Two-Year Colleges; Office Technology/Secretarial Educators of SUNY; and Alpha Xi Chapter of Delta Pi Epsilon, the honorary graduate business education society. Her other professional activities are numerous and include the Executive Board of the Business Education Association of Metropolitan New York until 1998; the 1990 Awards Committee of Alpha Chapter, Delta Pi Epsilon; editor of the spring 1985, 1986, and 1987 BEA *Journal of the Business Education Association of Metropolitan New York;* editorial board member of *Educational Dimensions,* the professional journal of The New York State Association of Two-Year Colleges; PLS Certifying Board member of the National Association of Legal Secretaries; National Council Delegate of Alpha Xi Chapter, Delta Pi Epsilon; and program co-chair of the 1986 Annual Conference of the Eastern Business Education Association. She is also a member of the Business Teachers Association, the National Business Education Association, International Society of Business Education, and Phi Delta Kappa.

The author was the recipient in 1982 of the prestigious Delta Pi Epsilon National Research Award. Other honors bestowed upon her in recognition of her leadership, scholarship, and contributions to the field of business education include: 1992 Outstanding Business Educator award of the Business Education Association of Metropolitan New York; 1987 EBEA Educator-of-the-Year; 1987 Outstanding Member Award of The New York State Association of Two-Year Colleges; 1982 Paul S. Lomax Award (Alpha Chapter, New York University); 1979 Estelle L. Popham Award (Alpha Xi Chapter, Hunter College); and 1977 Certificate of Recognition (New York State Association of Two-Year Colleges). She also is listed in *Who's Who in the East, Foremost Women of the Twentieth Century, Who's Who in American Education, Who's Who in the World,* and *Dictionary of International Biography.*

Among her books (some with coauthors) are *Machine Transcription: Applied Language Skills,* third edition (1999); *Medical*

Transcription (1998); *Communication for the Workplace: An Integrated Language Approach* (1997); *Opportunities in Office Occupations* (1995); *Opportunities in Customer Service* (1992); *Keyboarding Proficiency Drillbook* (1988); and *Time-It! Drillbook* (1988). *Communication for the Workplace: An Integrated Language Approach* won the Alpha Chapter (NYU), Delta Pi Epsilon Award for the best text of the year.

In addition to writing, Ettinger is an educational consultant. She conducts workshops and is a guest speaker, moderator, and panelist at many institutions as well as at annual conventions and professional meetings throughout the nation.